AMERICAN COUNTRY
CHRISTMAS
1996

Compiled and Edited by
Brenda Waldron Kolb
and Shannon Sexton Jernigan

©1996 by Oxmoor House, Inc.
Book Division of Southern Progress Corporation
P.O. Box 2463, Birmingham, Alabama 35201

Published by Oxmoor House, Inc., and Leisure Arts, Inc.

Library of Congress Catalog Card Number: 89-61909
ISBN: 0-8487-1519-5
ISSN: 1044-4904
Manufactured in the United States of America
First Printing 1996

Editor-in-Chief: Nancy Fitzpatrick Wyatt
Senior Homes Editor: Mary Kay Culpepper
Senior Foods Editor: Susan Carlisle Payne
Senior Editor, Editorial Services: Olivia Kindig Wells
Art Director: James Boone

AMERICAN COUNTRY CHRISTMAS 1996

Editor: Brenda Waldron Kolb
Assistant Editor: Shannon Sexton Jernigan
Recipe Editor: Lisa Hooper Talley
Editorial Assistant: Laura A. Fredericks
Copy Editors: Donna Baldone, Susan S. Cheatham
Assistant Art Director: Cynthia R. Cooper
Designer: Melissa Jones Clark
Director, Test Kitchens: Kathleen Royal Phillips
Assistant Director, Test Kitchens: Gayle Hays Sadler
Test Kitchens Home Economists: Susan Hall Bellows,
    Julie Christopher, Michele Brown Fuller, Heather Irby,
    Natalie E. King, Elizabeth Tyler Luckett, Jan Jacks Moon,
    Iris Crawley O'Brien, Jan A. Smith
Senior Photographer: John O'Hagan
Photographer: Ralph Anderson
Photo Stylists: Virginia R. Cravens, Katie Stoddard
Production and Distribution Director: Phillip Lee
Associate Production Managers: Theresa L. Beste,
    Vanessa D. Cobbs
Production Coordinator: Marianne Jordan Wilson
Production Assistant: Valerie L. Heard
Illustrator: Kelly Davis
Senior Production Designer: Larry Hunter
Publishing Systems Administrator: Rick Tucker

Table linens, page 20

COUNTRY CHRISTMAS AT HOME
4

Settle in with a generous menu
of simple-to-make decorations.

HOLIDAY HANDIWORK
30

Whether you paint, stamp, or sew,
you'll find something to love in our projects
for gift giving and tree trimming.

Ornaments, page 72

TREASURED TRADITIONS
54

Make everything old new again with ornaments and fabulous pound cakes.

PLEASURES OF THE SEASON
110

For a fine finish, check out ideas for creating a Christmas you'll remember.

Syrup, page 83

COUNTRY CHRISTMAS PANTRY
78

Rely on these kitchen-tested recipes for quick gifts and easy entertaining.

Reindeer, page 114

Tubby Topiaries, page 18

COUNTRY CHRISTMAS AT HOME

Get into the spirit with crafts designed to warm the home. *Embellishing* purchased wreaths and doormats is a quick way to create outdoor *decorations.* Extending the cheer all through the house is as easy as picking *your favorite* technique—crafting boxwood topiaries, sewing a wool throw, or mixing up bowls of potpourri.

SKIRT THE TREE IN *Style*

Join squares of crimson and gold velvet and trim the whole with two-tone fringe. The result is a tree skirt that's both classy and a bit splashy.

Materials:
1 yard 54"-wide red upholstery velvet
1 yard 54"-wide gold upholstery velvet
1½ yards 54"-wide plaid fabric
Pushpin
String
5½ yards 1½"-wide red-and-gold
    eyelash fringe
4 coat hook-and-eye closures
Thread to match fabrics

Note: All seam allowances are ½". Place nap of velvet in same direction when cutting. Finished size is approximately 47½" square (excluding fringe). For eyelash fringe, see source listing on page 156.

1. Cut out fabric. From red velvet, cut 4 (17") squares.

From gold velvet, cut 3 (17") squares and 2 (17¾") squares. Cut 17¾" gold squares in half diagonally to make 4 triangles.

For backing, cut a 49¾" square from plaid fabric. Cut square in half diagonally to make 2 triangles.

2. Cut out center opening. To make a compass, tie 1 end of string to pushpin and other end to pencil, making sure string in between measures 3½". Place 1 gold triangle wrong side up. Referring to Diagram A, insert pushpin in center of diagonal edge of triangle. Holding string taut, mark half-circle as shown. Cut out along traced line. Repeat on a second gold triangle.

Repeat to mark and cut out center half-circles in plaid backing triangles.

Diagram A

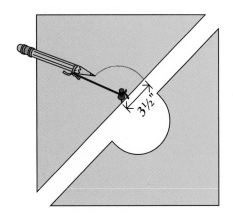

3. Assemble top. With right sides facing, join velvet pieces as shown to make Units A, B, and C (Diagram B). Join Unit A to Unit B along short diagonal seam only. Staystitch ½" from edge around center circle and long diagonal opening. Join Unit C to top edge of A/B unit.

4. Assemble backing. With right sides facing and raw edges aligned, stitch plaid triangles together from edge of center opening to 1 corner, leaving remaining diagonal edge open.

Diagram B

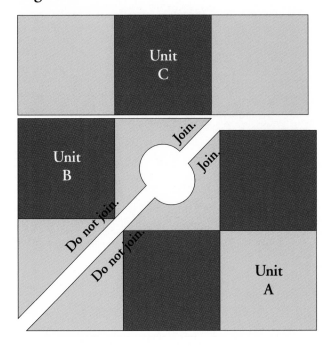

5. Add fringe. Place pieced top right side up. Beginning and ending at diagonal edge, align bound edge of fringe with raw edge of pieced top, with fringe toward center. Pin fringe in place, easing around corners. Baste fringe ½" from bound edge, beginning and ending ½" from each end. Backstitch to secure seam.

6. Stitch top to backing. With right sides facing, raw edges aligned, and fringe sandwiched between, stack top and backing; pin. Stitch along all raw edges, leaving a 10" opening in 1 diagonal edge for turning. Trim fabric close to seam (do not cut bound edge of fringe). Clip seams around center circle and corners. Turn right side out. Press, if necessary, being careful not

to crush nap. Slipstitch opening closed.

    7. **Add closures.** Along diagonal opening, stitch hook-and-eye closures in place, spacing them evenly.

STORAGE TIP. To prevent nap of velvet from being crushed, store tree skirt by wrapping it around a cardboard roll.

Manteled

IN WHITE

For this no-sew drape, all you do is blanket your mantel in billows of snowy fabric.

Materials:

White net or lace figured with stars or holiday motifs
   (see Note and Step 1 below)
7 yards 1½"-wide white-and-gold sheer ribbon
Straight pins

  Note: For sources for figured net and also for figured laces, see page 156.

  1. Cut net and ribbon. Measure length of mantel and add 36" (for an 18" drop at each end). Measure width of mantel and add 18" (for drop at front). Using selvage as 1 long edge, cut net to these measurements. (Our drape fits a 45"-long mantel and requires 2¼ yards of net.) For ties, cut ribbon into 7 (1-yard) lengths.

  2. Mark placement for ties. Place net on mantel, aligning selvage with back of mantel. Adjust net so that drop is 18" on front and both sides. Place several books on top to hold net in place.

  Insert straight pins in net to mark each corner of mantel (2 in front, 2 in back). On front edge of mantel, mark center. On each side of center mark, mark point midway between center and corner (total of 7 pins).

  3. Gather and tie drape. Using sharp pencil, make small holes in net at marked points. Remove pins.

  Referring to photograph, thread 1 ribbon tie halfway through each hole. Tie each ribbon into a bow, gathering net to form a swag. At each front corner of mantel, fold under corner of net and secure with ribbon bow, arranging net as shown.

FIVE *Welcome* WREATHS

To give plain wreaths a natural charm, dress them up with leaves, flowers, and other bountiful botanicals.

An evergreen wreath is one of the season's most familiar symbols. A wreath on the front door is a traditional way of welcoming holiday visitors. A wreath over a mantel or on a mirror is a fragrant means of bringing the cheer indoors. In the last few years, we've even seen wreaths adorning automobiles—a new twist on outdoor decor.

This year, instead of relying on the familiar green-wreath-with-a-red-bow combo, display a wreath whose natural embellishments give it a certain grace.

Each of the five wreaths that follow illustrates the effectiveness of this technique. Here are a few tips on getting started.

• **Sources for wreaths.** Christmas tree lots often carry wreaths (as well as garlands and loose greenery). Other sources are local chapters of the Boy Scouts and service organizations.

If you're an urban dweller, or if you simply like the convenience of having a wreath delivered to your door, purchase one by mail. We ordered our 26" wreaths (seen on the opposite and following pages) from a tree farm in North Carolina; to order your own, see page 156.

• **Sources for natural materials.** Although we've listed how many of each item we used in our wreaths, you can use as little or as much you like. Naturals are sold by florist's shops, the floral departments of crafts stores, or the source listed on page 156.

If you can't find a certain item, substitute something your store does carry or—better yet—something you clip from your yard. Such creative exchanges often result in a fresh, spontaneous look.

And remember: Once you've finished displaying the wreath, you can detach the embellishments and save them for use in other projects.

• **Tips for hanging your wreath.** If you want to add a bow as a finishing touch, consider using some of the ribbon as a hanger, too. (For tips on tying bows, see pages 62–65.)

A wreath hung indoors will scent your rooms with its clean, sharp fragrance. On the other hand, a wreath hung outdoors will remain fresh for many weeks and even months in some climates.

Pinecones and Eucalyptus *The dense foliage of Fraser fir is forgiving, allowing the glue and wire to be easily hidden.*

Materials:
Fresh Fraser fir wreath
Eucalyptus pods
Pinecones
Acorns
Florist's wire
Hot-glue gun and glue sticks

1. **Attach materials.** Using florist's wire, tuck eucalyptus pods around wreath. Arrange pinecones in bunches of 3 and hot-glue around wreath. Hot-glue acorns around wreath.

Pinecones and Eucalyptus

Larkspur and Paperwhites

Larkspur and Paperwhites *If you can't find dried larkspur, you can dry fresh larkspur by hanging the stalks upside down for two weeks.*

Materials:
Fresh Fraser fir wreath
3 bunches dried white larkspur
3 paperwhite bulbs
1 yard 1½"-wide sheer white ribbon
Florist's wire

1. **Attach larkspur.** Using short lengths of florist's wire, attach sprigs of dried larkspur around center of wreath.

2. **Attach paperwhite bulbs.** Run wire through back of each paperwhite bulb and attach securely to bottom of wreath.

3. **Add bow.** Tie ribbon in a bow and wire bow to wreath.

Protea and Pepper Berries *You can find protea flowers and pepper berries at florist's shops and large crafts stores. Try this technique for softening pepper berries and other delicate materials so that they can be pulled apart more easily: Hold them over steam for a minute before removing them from the cellophane wrapping.*

Materials:
Fresh Scotch pine wreath
2 protea flowers
Pepper berries
Eucalyptus leaves
Salal leaves
Florist's wire
Hot-glue gun and glue sticks

1. **Attach materials.** Run lengths of florist's wire through protea flowers and attach to bottom center of wreath. Hot-glue bunches of pepper berries, eucalyptus leaves, and salal leaves around protea, hiding stems.

Protea and Pepper Berries

Fresh Heather

Fresh Heather
If you hang this wreath indoors, the purple heather will outlast the Scotch pine by several weeks. After we took our wreath down, we placed the heather in a glass vase for a quick centerpiece.

Materials:
Fresh Scotch pine wreath
2 bunches fresh heather
Sprigs of fresh rosemary (optional)
Florist's wire

1. **Attach heather.** Using short lengths of florist's wire, attach sprigs of heather to wreath, spacing heather sprigs evenly around wreath.
2. **Attach rosemary.** If desired, attach sprigs of rosemary as described in Step 1.

Gilded Accents
For a natural look, we applied the gold spray paint with a light touch. If you want more contrast between the greens and golds, spray on a heavier coat of paint.

Materials:
Fresh boxwood wreath
2 artichokes
Lotus pod
Salal leaves
Gold spray paint
Florist's wire
Hot-glue gun and glue sticks
Raffia

1. **Paint materials.** Spritz artichokes, lotus pod, and salal leaves with gold spray paint. Let dry.
2. **Attach materials.** Using florist's wire, attach artichokes and lotus pod to bottom as shown. Hot-glue salal leaves around wreath. Tie raffia bow at top.

Gilded Accents

THREE *Throws* THAT
ARE SIMPLE TO SEW

Bind a square of wool coating, perhaps embroider
the corners or edges, and you'll have a warm,
good-looking throw to give or keep.

True Blue

Materials for 1 throw:
1⅝ yards 54"-wide blue wool coating,
   trimmed to measure 50" to 54" wide
13 yards ½"-wide folded binding, pressed flat
Thread to match binding

1. Prepare binding. Measure length of 1 edge of throw, multiply by 2, and add 5". Cut 4 lengths of binding to this measurement.

Fold 1 binding length in half, matching short ends and aligning long edges. Topstitch through both layers just inside 1 long edge, backstitching at beginning and end. Repeat for 3 remaining binding lengths.

2. Attach binding. Encase raw edge of 1 side of throw in fold of 1 binding length, positioning folded end of binding almost flush with 1 corner of throw; pin. Trim raw ends of binding flush with other corner.

Pin next binding length to adjacent side, covering raw ends of previous length with folded end of second length. Repeat with 2 remaining sides, tucking raw ends of last binding length into folded end of first length. Topstitch binding just inside both long edges, catching all layers in seam and pivoting at corners.

Crimson and Cross-stitch

Materials for 1 throw:
1⅝ yards 54"-wide red wool coating,
   trimmed to measure 50" to 54" square
13 yards ½"-wide folded binding, pressed flat
Thread to match binding
1 skein red #3 pearl cotton
Large-eyed embroidery needle

1. Make throw. Repeat Steps 1–2 for True Blue.

2. Cross-stitch corners. For each double-sided, 1"-wide cross-stitch, thread needle with 1 yard of pearl cotton; knot end. At corner, insert needle in top layer of binding, 1" away from where stitch begins. Run needle

between layers and bring it up where stitch begins. Tug thread to pull knot through, hiding it under binding.

Stitch each leg 4 times. For first leg, stitch through both binding layers. Running needle between layers, bring needle up for second leg; stitch leg 3 times. To end, measure last leg and knot thread just beyond this point. Stitch last leg, running needle between layers and bringing needle up 1" away. Tug thread to pull knot through; trim thread.

Winter White

Materials for 1 throw:
1⅝ yards 54"-wide cream wool coating,
   trimmed to measure 50" to 54"square
13 yards ½"-wide folded binding, pressed flat
Thread to match binding
3 skeins #3 cream pearl cotton
Large-eyed embroidery needle

1. Make throw. Repeat Steps 1–2 for True Blue.

2. Embroider edges. Thread needle with 2–3 yards of pearl cotton. Embroider only top layer of binding, beginning and ending threads as described in Step 2 of Crimson and Cross-stitch.

At each corner, work 3 lazy daisy stitches, referring to Diagram below and to diagram on page 140.

Along each edge, work modified chevron stitches, referring to Diagram below. Bring needle up at A; backstitch. Go down at B, up at C, down at D, and so on, finishing in an "up" positon; backstitch. Work 1 lazy daisy stitch between each chevron stitch, running needle between layers to make a straight stitch over each leg of chevron stitch.

Diagram

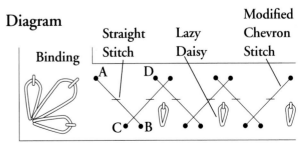

Tubby TOPIARIES

Perk up a mantel or tabletop with these pint-sized Christmas trees. During the winter, the heated air in most homes will slowly dry the boxwood and preserve the trees for months.

Materials:

Styrofoam cone: 21"-high cone for 5"–7" topiary, or 25"-high cone for 9" topiary (see Note below)

Green spray paint

5"-square Styrofoam block

5"-diameter x 4¼"-high terra-cotta flowerpot

6"-long ¼"-diameter wooden dowel

Hot-glue gun and glue sticks

12" boxwood cuttings: 2 dozen for 5"–7" topiary, or 3 dozen for 9" topiary

U-shaped florist's pins

Trims: crinkle wire, charms, small ornaments, or other trims (see Note below)

Note: Topiary height refers to tree only. For trims and boxwood, see sources on page 156.

1. Make base. Measure Styrofoam cone from bottom to desired height of topiary. Using knife, cut off top; discard. Trim new top to a thick point. Paint cone green; let dry.

Trim Styrofoam block to fit snugly in pot. With dowel, make 3"-deep hole in center of block in pot and also in center of cone bottom. Fill holes and cover cone bottom with hot glue. Insert half of dowel into cone; insert other end in block.

2. Add boxwood. Trim cuttings to 6"–8" lengths. Starting at base of cone and working horizontally in 1 direction, use florist's pins to attach cuttings. When 2" of cone remains at top, begin placing cuttings vertically to form a point, overlapping and trimming as needed.

3. Add trims. Decorate topiary as desired.

Flowering FLEECE

For a table blooming with Christmas color, whip up these polar-fleece perennials. The place mats are quickly blanket-stitched, while the napkin rings require no sewing at all.

Place Mats

Materials for 4:
¾ yard each 60"-wide polar fleece: red, green
1 skein each #3 pearl cotton: red, green
Large-eyed embroidery needle

1. **Cut out place mats.** From red fleece, cut 4 (13" x 18") pieces. From green fleece, cut 4 (13" x 18") pieces.

2. **Stitch place mats.** For each red place mat: Stack 2 red pieces, aligning edges; pin. Thread needle with green pearl cotton; knot end. Referring to Diagram, use ½"-long blanket stitches to join layers along all edges, hiding knots between layers. Repeat to make 2 green place mats with red pearl cotton.

Diagram

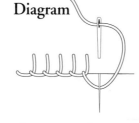

Napkin Rings

Materials for 4:
Patterns on pages 136–37
Tracing paper
¼ yard each 60"-wide polar fleece: red, green (or scraps left over from place mats)

1. **Cut out pieces.** Using tracing paper, transfer patterns to fleece. For each napkin ring, cut out 1 red flower piece and 2 green leaf pieces.

2. **Fold rings.** For each napkin ring, fold 1 flower in half, inserting solid end of petals through hole at opposite end.

3. **Finish rings.** For each napkin ring, stack 2 leaf pieces, aligning holes. Insert flower petals through hole in leaves. Adjust petals and leaves as desired. Insert napkin through ring.

Making Your Napkin Rings Bloom

Step 1

Step 2

Step 3

FRONT DOOR
Greetings

Stencil a friendly forest on a natural-fiber mat, and bring the holidays right up to your door. Using spray paints makes the stenciling simple.

Materials:
Patterns on page 138
Tracing paper
Natural-fiber outdoor mat
Sheet of paper cut same size as mat
Carbon paper
3 sheets of posterboard cut same size as mat
Protective mat or large piece of cardboard
Craft knife
Clear acrylic spray finish
Spray paints: yellow, light green, dark green
Large-tip white paint pen

1. **Transfer patterns.** Using tracing paper, transfer patterns to large sheet of paper, referring to Diagram on page 138 for placement. (Placement needn't be exact.) Designate some trees light green and some dark green.

2. **Make stencils.** Using carbon paper, transfer stars from paper to 1 posterboard sheet. Using protective mat and craft knife, cut out stencil for stars. Repeat to make 1 stencil for light green trees and 1 for dark green trees.

3. **Paint design.** Spray mat with acrylic finish; let dry. Place light green tree stencil on mat and spray with light green paint. (Spray in short bursts; continuous spraying causes paint to run.) Remove stencil; let dry.

Repeat to stencil dark green trees and then stars, letting paint dry between steps.

Using white paint pen, randomly paint snowflakes on several trees; let dry.

Jingle
ALL THE WAY

Glue silver bells to burlap covers, and turn a potted plant into a gift that sings.

Materials:
Holiday plant in plastic pot (see Note below)
Tracing paper
String and pushpin
1 yard burlap: red, cream, or green
Hot-glue gun and glue sticks
13-mm and 20-mm silver jingle bells

Note: If pot has a foil wrapper, trim it even with top edge of pot. If not, wrap pot in plastic wrap or aluminum foil, securing wrap with masking tape.

1. Cut out fabric. To determine diameter for wrapper, measure from inside of pot at soil line, up over top of pot, down and around pot, to opposite side soil line. Tape sheets of paper together to make a square equal to diameter. Fold paper in half and then in fourths.

To make pattern, divide diameter in half to find radius. Tie 1 end of string to pushpin and other end to pencil, making sure that string in between equals radius. Insert pushpin at folded corner of paper. Pulling string taut, draw an arc from edge to edge. Cut out pattern. Place pattern on burlap and cut out.

2. Glue wrapper to pot. Center pot on burlap. Pull burlap up, fold excess over rim, and glue to inside edge of pot just above soil line. Continue around pot, pleating as necessary to ease fullness.

3. Add bells. Glue or sew bells in place.

Citrus Containers
(For instructions, see page 28.)

MAKE *Good* SCENTS

Each of these enticing potpourris has several uses and packaging options. Whatever you choose, your success is sure to be sweet.

Citrus and Spice Potpourri

Citrus and Spice Potpourri *This piquant blend is perfect for the holidays. To make the spirals, use a citrus zester to cut long strips of peel. Wrap the strips around your finger to shape them, and let them air-dry. Another option is to use a sharp knife to cut the peel into simple shapes or short strips. You can order spices and essential oil from the sources listed on page 156.*

Ingredients for 3 cups:
1 cup broken cinnamon sticks (1" pieces)
4 whole nutmegs
½ cup each: star anise, cardamom pods, whole allspice
    berries, and dried orange, grapefruit, or lemon peel
2–3 drops essential oil of orange (optional)

Mix all ingredients in a large bowl. Stir well. Store in an airtight container, or package for gift giving.

Winter Forest Potpourri *Gathering these ingredients is a great excuse for taking the afternoon off and walking in the woods. If pinewoods aren't abundant in your region, substitute other leaves, berries, or seed pods. You'll find juniper berries, rose hips, and essential oil at health food stores and the sources listed on page 156.*

Use Winter Forest Potpourri to craft scented decorations or ornaments by gluing the mixture onto Styrofoam shapes or papier-mâché balls. Or, for fireside fragrance, toss a handful of potpourri on the flames.

Ingredients for 4 cups:
2 cups pine needles (reserve a few large sprigs for
    decoration)
1 cup pinecone scales or small pinecones
½ cup juniper berries
½ cup rose hips
2–3 drops essential oil of pine (optional)

Mix all ingredients in a large bowl. Stir well. Store in an airtight container, or package for gift giving.

Winter Forest Potpourri

Bower of Flowers Potpourri

Combine pink, yellow, and lavender flowers for a feminine mix. For the ingredients, dry your own garden's harvest, check out your local health food stores, or consult the sources listed on page 156. You can even use the contents of chamomile and jasmine tea bags, provided they contain 100% flowers—read the labels to make sure.

For an invigorating bath, run the water over a tea ball or cotton bag filled with the mixture and hung from the faucet. Or fill a crystal bowl or candy dish with the potpourri, and place it on a bedside table in the guest room.

Ingredients for 3 cups:
1 vanilla bean
1 cup rosebuds or rose petals
1 cup lavender flowers
½ cup chamomile flowers
½ cup jasmine flowers
2–3 drops of essential oil of lavender or chamomile
   (optional)

Cut the vanilla bean into small pieces with scissors. Mix all ingredients in a large bowl. Stir well. Store in an airtight container, or package for gift giving.

Finish with a Flourish

Janice Cox is one of the most creative people we know. After concocting the potpourri recipes featured here, she came up with these clever packaging ideas.

Citrus Containers

Cut off the top third of an orange, grapefruit, or pomelo. From both sections, scrape out all of the fruit and as much of the pith as you can. Rinse the sections with cool water and let dry. To dry the sections until they harden, dehydrate them in a food dehydrator, or bake them in the oven on the lowest setting (about 125° for 8–12 hours, turning occasionally on rack), or air-dry them in a warm, sunny place. (Janice's best results were with the food dehydrator, but any of these methods work.) Fill the citrus container with potpourri, place the lid on top, and tie it up with raffia. Decorate with bay leaves, cinnamon sticks, and star anise (see page 26).

Muslin Sachet Bags

Purchase or stitch plain muslin sachet bags. (Muslin bags like those shown on the facing page are found at kitchen and gourmet shops, where they're sold for use with bouquets garnis.) Embellish the bags with fabric paints or simple embroidery stitches. Fill the bag with a ¼ cup or so of potpourri.

Potpourri Packages

For a simple and practical way to give potpourri, just fill a zip-top plastic bag with the mixture and criss-cross the bag with raffia, tying it as you would ribbon on a package.

For the gift tags, gather the largest bay leaves you can find and use a hole punch to perforate them at one end. With a gold or silver paint pen, write your message on the tops of the leaves. To attach them, thread raffia through the holes and tie the tags to the packages. Use an embosser to personalize a brown craft-paper gift tag.

Potpourri Packages

Muslin Sachet Bags

Wire stars, page 40;
star garland, page 32.

HOLIDAY HANDIWORK

We designed this collection
of crafts to meet all of your
seasonal needs. Start with making
star-struck
decorations of wire and wood.
Then embellish linens or
embroider sachets
for presents you'll take pride
in. And for something that's
fun to wear,
our cardigans, nightgowns, and
slippers have you covered.

Great GARLANDS!

Begin with colored wooden beads; it's a head start on painting plain ones. Strand the beads with a darning needle threaded with cotton string. And involve your family in the painting and stringing. That way, you'll make quick work of your garlands— and make warm memories, too.

Stringing Stars

Hot-glue 1½" star cutouts to 8-mm round beads. String stars and ⅝" square beads, spacing them as shown at left. To secure beads, apply hot-glue inside each bead hole, or knot string on both sides of each bead.

Painterly Touches I

Paint assorted ½"- to ¾"-wide beads with polka dots and dashes. (**Tip:** To paint, anchor bead on point of a pencil. Place painted bead, still on pencil, in small glass to dry.) Spray with clear acrylic finish. String beads end to end, as shown at right.

Painterly Touches I

Stringing Stars

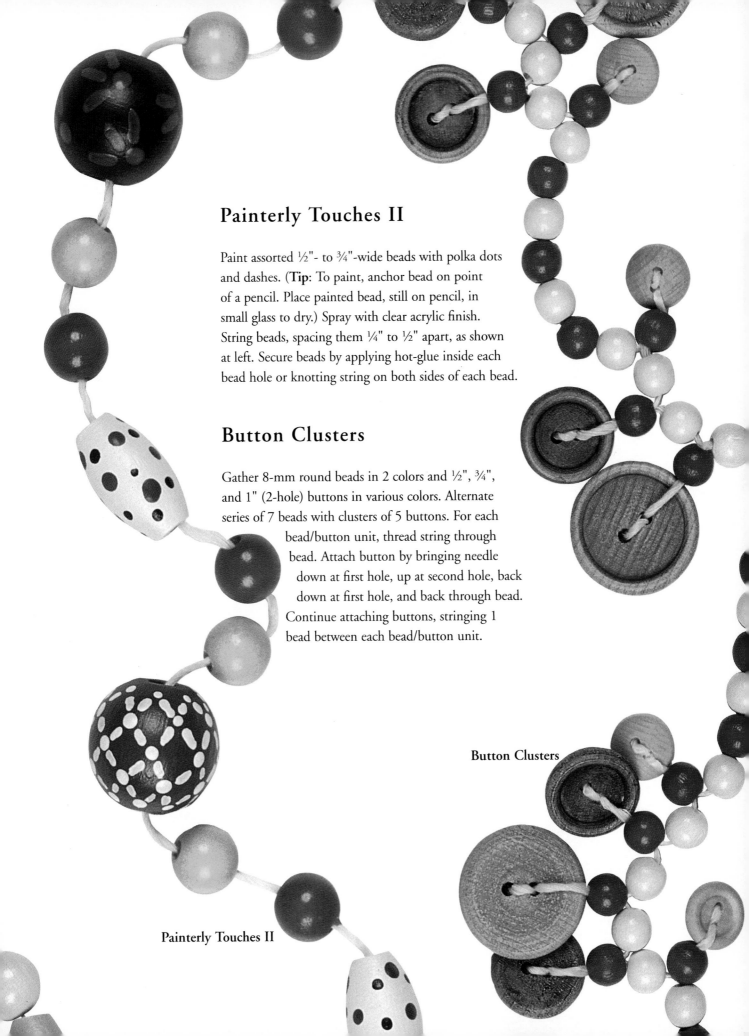

Painterly Touches II

Paint assorted ½"- to ¾"-wide beads with polka dots and dashes. (**Tip:** To paint, anchor bead on point of a pencil. Place painted bead, still on pencil, in small glass to dry.) Spray with clear acrylic finish. String beads, spacing them ¼" to ½" apart, as shown at left. Secure beads by applying hot-glue inside each bead hole or knotting string on both sides of each bead.

Button Clusters

Gather 8-mm round beads in 2 colors and ½", ¾", and 1" (2-hole) buttons in various colors. Alternate series of 7 beads with clusters of 5 buttons. For each bead/button unit, thread string through bead. Attach button by bringing needle down at first hole, up at second hole, back down at first hole, and back through bead. Continue attaching buttons, stringing 1 bead between each bead/button unit.

Button Clusters

Painterly Touches II

Puzzle KEEPER

This colorful roll-away mat safely holds an unfinished puzzle together and stores it for later.

Materials:
1 yard 45"-wide green cotton flannel
1 yard 45"-wide red pinwale corduroy
2 yards 1"-wide yellow grosgrain ribbon, cut in half
2 (2"-diameter x 44"-long) cardboard tubes
Yellow thread
Dressmaker's chalk

1. **Trim fabrics.** With wrong sides facing and raw edges aligned, stack fabrics. Trim edges so that pieces are same size. Separate fabrics.

2. **Attach ties.** Mark placement for ties on right side of corduroy. Topstitch 1 ribbon length over each mark (Diagram A).

Diagram A

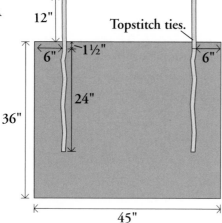

3. **Stitch casing edges.** On corduroy, make a mark 4" from each corner along both short edges. Zigzag each short edge from corner to mark, backstitching at beginning and end to reinforce.

Repeat on flannel.

4. **Stitch edges of mat.** With wrong sides facing and raw edges aligned, stack corduroy on flannel. Zigzag fabrics along long edges, keeping ties free.

Beginning and ending 4" from corners, zigzag fabrics along short edges, leaving casings open (Diagram B).

Diagram B

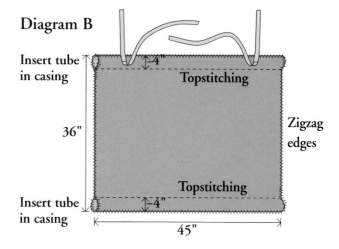

5. **Topstitch casings.** Using chalk, lightly mark a 4"-wide casing parallel to long edges. Topstitch along each marked line, keeping ties free (Diagram B).

6. **Finish mat.** Insert tubes in casings. Work puzzle on flannel side of mat. To store, roll from long end opposite ribbon ties. When tubes meet, wrap long ribbon end around both tubes to meet short ribbon; tie.

Puzzles by Post *The mail-order catalog* Bits & Pieces *proves that there's more to jigsaw puzzles than fuzzy photos and peeling pasteboard.*

While *Bits & Pieces* does sell traditional versions, it also offers such unusual fare as wooden puzzles and three-dimensional replicas of famous buildings. The holiday catalog has seasonal selections, including a Christmas tree that (with batteries) actually lights up. To order the catalog, turn to page 156.

Stamp ON THE Cheer

Trace holiday motifs onto foam trays, add ink or paint, and let the decorating begin.

Kitchen Towels

Materials for 1:
Patterns on page 139
Tracing paper
Unused foam food tray
Ballpoint pen with cap
Masking tape
Cotton kitchen towel
Ink pad: red, green, or blue
Pressing cloth
Iron
Embroidery needle
Red embroidery floss

1. **Make stamp.** Using tracing paper, trace desired pattern. Place pattern on flat area of tray. Retrace pattern lines, pressing firmly to imprint design into foam. Remove pattern. Referring to box on page 139, use pen with cap to make a positive or a negative stamp. Cut foam just outside design area. For handle, attach a 3"–4" length of tape to wrong side of stamp as shown in Diagram below.

Diagram

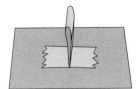

2. **Stamp towel.** Press stamp on ink pad several times. For border, stamp approximately 1½" from bottom edge, beginning at 1 long edge and repeating stamp across width of towel. Reink stamp after each use. If desired, stamp only 1 image in center, as shown on red-stamped towel in photograph on pages 36–37. Let dry.

3. **Heat-set ink.** Cover stamped design with pressing cloth. Using hot iron, press several seconds to set ink.

4. **Outline design.** Thread needle with 2 or 3 strands of floss. Hiding knots on wrong side of towel, make running stitches ¼" from outer edges of design.

Gift Tags

Materials:
Patterns on page 139
Tracing paper
Unused foam food tray
Ballpoint pen with cap
Masking tape
Ink pads: red, green, blue
Tie-on package tags
Craft knife (optional)

1. **Make stamp.** Repeat Step 1 for Kitchen Towels (page 37).

2. **Stamp tags.** Press stamp on ink pad several times. For border, stamp across bottom edge of tag. For single motif, stamp randomly on 1 side of tag. Let dry.

Stamp-ease *Follow these hints for finding proper materials and achieving pleasing results.*

A good source. Ask your butcher for clean, unused foam trays; ours was happy to give us a few for free.

Cutting corners. Cut the curved sides off each foam tray, saving the flat parts for making your stamps.

Bold impressions. For a more pronounced design, trace the pattern lines twice—once with tracing paper in place (to transfer the design), and then once again without the tracing paper (to make a deeper impression).

Test run. Before you begin your project, experiment by stamping on scrap paper. Evenly distribute the ink on your stamp and replenish the ink after each impression.

A clean break. Press the stamp firmly and then lift it straight up from the surface. Avoid dragging or twisting the stamp, which will smudge the ink.

Consider this. Tags and towels are only two of the many items you can stamp. Other possibilities include frames, blank books, cotton T-shirts or sweatshirts, stationery, solid-color wrapping paper, and flat-sided accessories like boxes or trays.

Use a photocopier to enlarge or reduce the patterns as needed to suit the items to be decorated. Stamp the design in ink, acrylic paints, or fabric paints—whatever works best for the piece you choose.

Heavenly
METAL

Flexible craft wire is so easy to work with, you can create these stars in a twinkling. Make a large one to top the tree and then a constellation of smaller ones for ornaments.

Materials for 1 star:
Pattern on page 147
Tracing paper
Wood scrap
10 nails
Hammer
Needle-nosed pliers
20-gauge craft wire: silver, gold (for source, see page 156)
Wire cutters
Monofilament for ornament hanger

2. Form star. Wind silver wire around nails as shown, using pliers to make sharp corners and outlining star 4 times. Cut excess wire. To secure, tuck wire ends between other wires. Remove star from board.

1. Prepare board. Using tracing paper, transfer desired star pattern to wood. Drive a nail into each star point and inner corner, leaving ½" of nail exposed.

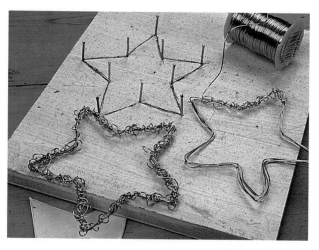

3. Finish star. Treating silver wires as 1 unit, wrap gold wire around star, forming loose spirals and loops. Cut excess wire and secure ends as described in Step 2. For ornament, cut a 9" length of monofilament. Loop through top of star and knot ends.

Ornament Star

A STITCHER'S
Gift

**This teacher, author, and fiber artist is eager to spread the word:
Silk ribbon embroidery is a stitch in time for today's crafters.**

For Judith Baker Montano, reviving the art of silk ribbon embroidery is a labor of love.

"Not only is the technique fast and effective," she says, "but it is also delicate and pretty." And as her students on three continents now know, it is easy to learn.

From quilts to silks. "I discovered silk ribbon embroidery years ago while teaching quilting classes in Australia," Judith explains. An expert on crazy quilts, she had written *The Crazy Quilt Handbook* and *Crazy Quilt Odyssey,* still leading texts in the field.

As Judith learned, silk ribbon embroidery began in 17th-century France. The fashion emigrated first to England and then to British-held colonies. Its popularity has waxed and waned through the years, but today new interest in the art is growing. Recalls Judith, "I was fascinated with the dimensional effect of the ribbon and what it added to crazy quilting." Convinced that others would also love stitching in silk, Judith began teaching it at events like Dollywood's annual American Quilt Showcase. Soon she was writing about the technique, too.

Ribbon recognition. Crafters praise Judith's latest books, *The Art of Silk Ribbon Embroidery* and *Elegant Stitches.* She is also busy creating a videotape series demonstrating silk ribbon embroidery, crazy quilting, and embellishing. For the past 12 years, her teaching has taken her across the United States and around the world, making Judith's one of the most recognizable names in needlework.

To learn more, you can order her books and videos from the source listed on page 156, or you can simply keep reading. In the following pages Judith presents a miniworkshop on silk ribbon embroidery.

Before You Begin *Most craft and needlework stores carry all the items you'll need for silk ribbon embroidery, but you can also order them from the source listed on page 156. Following are some things to keep in mind when you purchase your supplies.*

Fabrics. When you select your fabric, consider how you will use your embroidery—as clothing, jewelry, or a framed piece, for example.

For clothing that may receive a lot of wear, choose fabrics such as cottons, linens, and polyesters. (Always prewash these fabrics according to manufacturer's instructions.) For special-occasion clothing that you won't mind having dry-cleaned, use silks and satins.

Smaller items, such as pins, sachets, or framed embroideries, may be worked on any of these fabrics, as well as moiré, velvet, and taffeta. Craft stores offer small packages of crêpe silk and moiré next to the silk ribbon.

Loose-weave fabrics and knits may need an additional stabilizing layer to keep the stitches in place. We chose flannel for the nightgown that Judith stitched for us (see pages 46–47), but she prefers to work on batiste or silk for most of her projects.

Ribbon. Silk ribbon is almost always Judith's first choice because of its pliability, softness, and range of colors.

You may also use polyester ribbon. Judith cautions that synthetic ribbon doesn't have the fine feel or look of silk, but she acknowledges that its washability makes it a sensible choice for wearables. She recommends a brand called Heirloom Sylk, which will not fray and is the most silklike of the synthetics (for a source listing, see page 156).

Needles. Keep on hand a variety of needles in different sizes. Chenille needles have large eyes and sharp points. Use them for working on heavy fabric or stitches that repeatedly pierce the fabric. Tapestry needles also have large eyes but have blunt points. Use these needles for pulling the ribbon between a previous stitch and the fabric to prevent snagging.

Pin

Materials:
Pattern on page 143
Oval brooch pin kit
8" square of white moiré
Water-soluble marker
Tracing paper
Iron-on transfer pencil
6" embroidery hoop
4-mm ribbon: 4 floral colors, 3 shades of green
Light green silk buttonhole twist for feather stitches (may substitute embroidery floss)
Needles: chenille, tapestry
Scraps: thin cardboard, batting
Thick craft glue

1. **Transfer pattern.** Place pin frame on moiré and mark inside edge with water-soluble marker. Using tracing paper and following manufacturer's instructions for pencil, transfer pattern inside marked oval.

2. **Stitch design.** Place moiré in hoop. Stitch, referring to pages 140–43 and alternating colors as desired.

3. **Finish pin.** Cut out design, adding ½" around marked oval. Cut cardboard to fit inside frame. Place small amount of batting on cardboard. Center design right side up on top. Glue raw edges of fabric to back. Run a bead of glue around back of frame and place frame on design. Glue pin closure to back of pin.

"The secret is keeping the *ribbon* flat and the stitches loose."

Sachet

Materials:

Pattern on page 142
Water-soluble marker
2 (8") squares white moiré
Iron-on transfer pencil
Tracing paper
6" embroidery hoop
Needles: chenille, tapestry
4-mm ribbon: 8 pastel colors, 4 shades of green
Green silk buttonhole twist for feather stitches
    (may substitute embroidery floss)
22" (1½"-wide) pregathered lace
Stuffing: potpourri, dried lavender flowers, or dried
    herbs
Thread to match fabric

Note: Finished design is 3½" x 5½" (excluding lace). All seam allowances are ¼".

1. Transfer pattern. Using water-soluble marker, mark a 3½" x 5½" rectangle on 1 piece of moiré. Trace sachet pattern onto tracing paper with iron-on transfer pencil. Referring to photograph, position pattern in 1 corner of fabric, about ½" inside marked lines. Following manufacturer's instructions for pencil, transfer pattern to moiré.

2. Stitch design. Place moiré in embroidery hoop. Referring to pages 140–42 and alternating colors as desired, stitch design.

3. Finish sachet. Remove design from hoop. Cut out design, adding ¼" all around marked lines, so that sachet top measures 4" x 6".

With raw edges aligned, baste lace to right side of sachet top.

From remaining fabric, cut a 4" x 6" piece for back. With right sides facing, raw edges aligned, and lace sandwiched between, stitch around all edges, leaving a 2" opening for turning. Clip corners and turn right side out. Stuff loosely. Slipstitch opening closed.

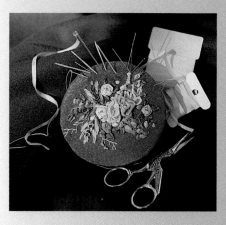

Master Strokes *For anyone who's held a needle, watching Judith embroider is an inspiration.*

With a few quick stitches, her nimble fingers transform narrow ribbon into a spray of flowers, a cluster of leaves, or a trailing vine. And she's quick to offer the following hints to those of us who are novices.

1. Decide on a color palette before beginning a project. Stick to pastels, dusty tones, or jewel tones.

2. Create a balance between warm and cool ribbon colors for a more interesting look.

3. Vary the greens in your work. "If you have five flower varieties, have five greens for the stems and leaves," she says.

4. Before you start working on a piece, purchase or gather all the supplies you'll need.

5. Mark the perimeter of your work on the fabric with a water-soluble marker.

6. Use a 6" embroidery hoop. Wrap the inside hoop with yarn to protect the fabric.

7. Prevent fraying by threading your needle with 12" lengths of ribbon.

8. Keep several needles threaded at a time.

9. For children's clothes or garments that will get lots of wear and tear, use whipstitches and knotted stitches like French knots.

10. Store materials and works-in-progress in zip-top plastic bags to keep your stitchery neat and clean.

A Historical Snippet *In her book* The Art of Silk Ribbon Embroidery, *Judith traces the elusive history of this stitching technique.*

It seems to have begun in 17th-century France as an elaborate embellishment to gowns worn by women of royalty. The fashion emigrated to England and then to British-held colonies.

In America, the introduction of French silk ribbon in 1870 began an interest in the art—and not only for clothing, but also for crazy quilts, hats, and household decorations.

Women in Australia embraced silk ribbon embroidery, too, using kits of patterns and ribbons from America and England.

Judith writes that the heyday of silk ribbon embroidery was in the 1880s and '90s. During those years, ladies' ball gowns and children's clothing were decorated with pastel ribbon motifs reminiscent of those used in France a century or two earlier. After 1900, however, interest in silk ribbon embroidery seemed to fade completely.

While pockets of interest in ribbon work around the world have remained strong, it wasn't until the 1980s that a noticeable revival began. Judith attributes the new popularity to Australian needleworkers who see the art as an important part of their culture and heritage. Whatever the source, silk ribbon embroidery's ease and opulence make it a wonderful choice for today's needleworker.

Nightgown

Materials:
Pattern on page 143
Purchased nightgown with plain bodice *or* nightgown pattern (we used Easy McCall's, #7951, View C) and required fabric (see Step 1)
Iron-on transfer pencil
Tracing paper
6" embroidery hoop
Needles: chenille, tapestry
4-mm ribbon: 9 pastel colors, 4 shades of green
Green silk buttonhole twist for feather stitches (may substitute embroidery floss)
Thread to match fabric

1. **Transfer pattern.** If using purchased nightgown, trace embroidery pattern onto tracing paper using iron-on transfer pencil. Following manufacturer's instructions for pencil, center and transfer pattern to nightgown.

If sewing nightgown, cut out pattern pieces. Place front pattern piece on fabric. Trace with water-soluble marker, marking seam lines and center. Do not cut out. Trace embroidery pattern onto tracing paper with iron-on transfer pencil. Following manufacturer's instructions for pencil, center and transfer pattern to fabric inside marked seam lines.

2. **Stitch design.** Place fabric in embroidery hoop. Referring to pages 140–43 and alternating colors as desired, stitch design.

3. **Finish nightown.** Following pattern instructions, cut out fabric and sew nightgown together.

"This is *heirloom* work, I tell my students—use the best materials you can afford."

Stylish SLIPPERS

**Surprise everyone from dad to baby brother with
a cushy pair of quick-stitch house shoes.**

Note: Patterns include ⅝" seam allowances. Yardages given for embellishments are for slippers shown in photograph; you may need more or less, depending on size you make.

Playful Polka

Materials for 1 pair:
Patterns on pages 144–45
⅓ yard 1"-thick foam
½ yard terry cloth in desired color
Dressmaker's pen
Thread to match fabric
16" (1"-wide) red fringe
10 (½") red pom-poms

1. **Cut slipper pieces.** Transfer desired patterns to fabric and foam and cut out as indicated on patterns. Using dressmaker's pen, label toe of each fabric piece. Trim ½" from edges of each foam piece and label toe.

2. **Make slipper tops.** With right sides facing and raw edges aligned, stitch 2 tops together along seam opposite toe (instep). Trim seam allowance, clip curves, and turn; press. Repeat to make top for second slipper.

3. **Assemble slippers.** With raw edges aligned, place 1 slipper top on right side of 1 slipper bottom at toe. Baste together along raw edges. With raw edges aligned, place second slipper bottom right side down on top of stack, with slipper top sandwiched between larger pieces. Using a ⅝" seam, stitch around outside edges through all layers, leaving 2" opening at heel. Turn slipper right side out through opening. Insert 1 piece of foam as shown in Diagram at right; whipstitch opening closed. Repeat to assemble second slipper.

4. **Embellish slippers.** Cut fringe in half. Stitch 1 length to each slipper top at instep as shown in Diagram above. Stitch 5 pom-poms to each slipper top.

Playful Polka

Sherpa Snugs

Twinkle Toes   Candy Canes

Sherpa Snugs

Materials for 1 pair:
Patterns on pages 144–45
⅓ yard 1"-thick foam
½ yard suede cloth in desired color
Dressmaker's pen
Thread to match fabric
⅓ yard synthetic sherpa

1. **Make slippers.** Repeat Steps 1–3 of Playful Polka.
2. **Embellish slippers.** Cut 2 (4" x 9") strips from sherpa. Fold cut ends under ½". Slipstitch edges of 1 strip to each slipper top at instep.

Twinkle Toes

Materials for 1 pair:
Patterns on pages 144–45
⅓ yard 1"-thick foam
½ yard terry cloth in desired color
Dressmaker's pen
Thread to match fabric
½ yard green medium rickrack
Shank buttons: 2 gold stars, 8 small red

1. **Make slippers.** Repeat Steps 1–3 of Playful Polka.
2. **Embellish slippers.** From rickrack, cut 3 (2½") strips for tree and 1 (1½") strip for tree trunk. Turn under cut ends and slipstitch pieces to slipper top as shown. Stitch 1 star and 4 red buttons in place. Repeat for second slipper.

Candy Canes

Materials for 1 pair:
Patterns on pages 144–45
⅓ yard 1"-thick foam
½ yard terry cloth in desired color
Dressmaker's pen
Thread to match fabric
⅝ yard each ⅛"-diameter silk cording: red, white

1. **Make slippers.** Repeat Steps 1–3 of Playful Polka.
2. **Embellish slippers.** From cording, cut 2 (6") strips and 2 (3") strips of each color. Knot 1 (6") strip of each color together at 1 end. Twist strips and knot other ends together. Slipstitch to slipper top at instep as shown in photograph. In same manner, twist 2 (3") strips together and slipstitch to slipper top to resemble candy cane. Repeat for second slipper.

CHRISTMAS
Cardigans

With our step-by-step instructions to keep you
moving, you can turn any plain sweatshirt into
a jazzy jacket for holiday outings.

Materials for 1 child's jacket:
1 red sweatshirt (see Note at right)
2 yards 1⅛"-wide blue embroidered ribbon
2½ yards ⅝"-wide green embroidered ribbon
2 yards blue double-fold quilt binding
3 yards blue extra-wide double-fold bias tape
5 yards green baby rickrack
5 yards white jumbo rickrack
Liqui-Fuse
Thread to match trims
20" red separating sport zipper
Purchased tassel or 1 skein each of pearl cotton:
    blue, red

Materials for 1 adult jacket:
1 green sweatshirt (see Note at right)
3 yards 1⅛"-wide red embroidered ribbon
4 yards ⅝"-wide blue embroidered ribbon
3 yards red double-fold quilt binding
3¼ yards red extra-wide double-fold bias tape
4 yards green baby rickrack
4 yards white jumbo rickrack
Liqui-Fuse
Thread to match trims
24" red separating sport zipper
Purchased tassel or 1 skein each pearl cotton:
    green, red

Note: Buy sweatshirt 1 size larger than usual. Jackets shown were made from child's size 14–16 and adult size XL. Yardages for other sizes may vary; see Step 1. Prewash sweatshirt and ribbons; then press ribbons.

1. **Measure sweatshirt.** To determine total length of trim units needed, measure around cuff; then measure across shirt front at chest between sleeve seams. Add these 2 measurements, add 3", and then double total.

2. **Cut trims.** Using above measurement, cut 1 length each of 1⅛" ribbon and quilt binding and 2 lengths each of baby and jumbo rickrack. Unfold binding. Cut in half along center fold; press flat.

3. **Make trim unit.** Following manufacturer's instructions, apply Liqui-Fuse to 1 long edge of 1 length of binding. Fuse 1 length of jumbo rickrack to binding. Repeat for remaining binding. Apply Liqui-Fuse to 1 long edge of 1⅛" ribbon. Fuse ribbon to 1 rickrack/binding unit (see photograph at left). Repeat on other ribbon edge. Fold under long outer edges of binding ⅜". Use Liqui-Fuse to attach lengths of baby rickrack just inside each folded edge of binding as shown. Using narrow zigzag, stitch along each edge of ribbon through all layers. Set aside.

4. **Remove ribbing.** On sweatshirt, cut narrow ribbing from neck and cuffs, leaving stitches to stabilize edges; discard ribbing. Remove stitches to take wide ribbing off bottom; set ribbing aside for collar.

5. **Attach trim to cuffs.** About 3" from sleeve end, measure around sleeve and add ½"; cut 2 trim units to match. Using ¼" seam and with right sides facing and raw edges aligned, stitch together ends of each trim to form a tube; turn. Slip trim on sleeve so that edge is 2" from cuff edge and seams are aligned; pin. Topstitch along center of baby rickrack. (If you do not have a free-arm machine, straightstitch rickrack after fusing in Step 3. Hand-stitch trim onto sleeve.) Finish cuff edges with double-fold bias tape, turning under raw ends.

6. **Attach trim across back.** Across shirt back, measure from sleeve seam to sleeve seam and add ½". Cut trim unit to this measurement. Pin trim in place, turning raw ends under ¼" and aligning folded ends with

seams. Slipstitch ends in place. Topstitch along center of each length of baby rickrack.

7. Attach trim to shoulders. Measure from 1 sleeve seam to neck edge and add ½". Cut 2 trim units to this measurement. Pin 1 trim unit to each shoulder, aligning top edge of trim with shoulder seam and turning raw ends under ¼". Slipstitch ends in place at seams. Topstitch down center of each length of baby rickrack.

8. Attach outside edge of collar. Cut center front of shirt open from neck to bottom edge. Measure around neck opening and add 1". Cut a length of wide ribbing to this measurement. Open ribbing and lay flat, leaving crease in center as a guideline.

With right sides facing and raw edges aligned, stitch 1 long edge of ribbing to neck edge. Trim excess ribbing. Press seam flat; then press seam allowance away from shirt.

9. Attach zipper. With right sides facing, place zipper along 1 edge of front opening, aligning top of pull with crease of collar ribbing. Using zipper foot, baste zipper.

Turn shirt to wrong side and baste zipper to opposite edge of front opening in same manner. Turn shirt to right side. Check that ribbing collar edges and bottom edges of shirt are even. Turn shirt to wrong side and stitch zipper in place along basting lines.

10. Finish collar. Refold ribbing along crease to make collar. Turn under raw edges and slipstitch binding to seam lines around neck and along zipper.

11. Attach ribbon to jacket front. Open jacket front. Cut ⅝"-wide embroidered ribbon in half. Apply Liqui-Fuse on front opening along 1 edge of zipper. Beginning at bottom edge of sweatshirt, fuse ribbon in place on jacket front. Continue to fuse ribbon over top of collar and along inside edge of zipper. Topstitch long ribbon edges through all layers. Repeat on other side.

12. Finish bottom edge. Measure around bottom edge of jacket and add ½". Cut a length of double-fold bias tape to match. Finish as for cuffs.

13. Attach tassel. Using pearl cotton, attach tassel to zipper pull. To make a tassel, see box below.

Tassels Without Hassles *If you can't find the right tassel at your fabric store, you can make your own from pearl cotton. Wash the floss before you use it to prevent it from bleeding onto other fabrics.*

Wrap pearl cotton around a 2½" cardboard square 40 times. Insert a 4" length of floss along the top edge of the cardboard; use this to tie the wound lengths together tightly. For the hanging loop, knot ends together. With scissors, clip the wound lengths along the bottom edge of the cardboard (Diagram A).

Cut a 36"-length from contrasting-colored floss. Make a ½"-long loop at 1 end of the contrasting length. Place loop near the top of the tassel (Diagram B).

Wrap the contrasting floss tightly around the tassel, working over the loop toward the top of the tassel to form a band approximately ¼" wide (Diagram C).

Thread the working end of the contrasting floss through the loop. Pull both ends of the floss tightly; the knot will slip behind the wrapped band of floss. Trim the ends even with the band. Smooth the tassel and trim the bottom ends even (Diagram D).

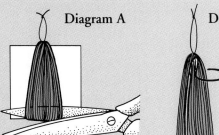
Diagram A

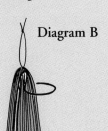
Diagram B

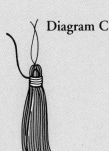
Diagram C

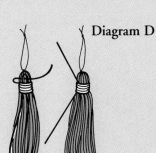
Diagram D

Stockings, page 66; ornaments, page 62.

TREASURED TRADITIONS

For a simpler, more satisfying holiday season, follow the *time-honored* custom of making your gifts and trimmings by hand. Some *smart solutions* are ornaments, stockings, and candles that take advantage of *today's fabrics* and materials. Or make the most of old Christmas cards— we give you eight great ideas.

Celestial CANDLES TO Light UP THE SEASON

Here are two bright ideas for holiday decorating and gift giving.
Use cookie cutters as molds for floating votives. Or start with ready-made
candles and simply stencil them with stars.

Floating Votives

Materials:
Baking pan at least 1" deep
Aluminum foil
Large coffee can
Paraffin wax, candle-making wax, or beeswax
½"-deep metal cookie cutters without backs: star, crescent moon
Skewer or chopstick
Candle wicking
Rub 'n' Buff gilding paste: gold, silver
Glitter: gold, silver

Note: Finished sizes of our star votives are 2" wide and 3" wide, and moon votive is 2½" long. Finished sizes of yours will depend on cookie cutters you use.

1. **Melt paraffin.** Line pan with foil, smoothing out any wrinkles in foil. Place coffee can in Dutch oven filled with several inches of water. Melt paraffin in coffee can over low heat. Pour melted paraffin into pan to a depth of about 1". Let paraffin cool until set but still slightly warm (about 1 to 1½ hours).

2. **Cut out votive shapes.** To cut out each star or moon shape, press sharp edge of cookie cutter into warm paraffin. Remove shape.

3. **Insert wicking.** With skewer, pierce center of warm votive. From bottom, thread wicking through hole, knotting or pressing wicking into wax at bottom. Clip wick ¼" above top. Let cool completely.

4. **Apply gilding paste.** Using fingers, apply gold or silver paste to surface of votive. Sprinkle with glitter.

Stenciled Candles

Materials:
Patterns on page 154
Tracing paper
Card stock or other heavyweight paper
Craft knife
Candles: 3" and 8" pillars, 8" tapers
Rub 'n' Buff gilding paste: gold, silver

1. **Prepare stencils.** Using tracing paper, transfer stencil patterns to card stock. Using craft knife, cut out stencils along pattern lines.

2. **Stencil candles.** On each candle, position stencil as desired and apply gilding paste with finger. Repeat as desired to stencil more star designs.

Wax Facts *Here's how to find the right wax for your candle-making projects.*

Paraffin. Paraffin is inexpensive, easy to work with, and widely available in grocery stores. A disadvantage is that paraffin candles don't burn as long as those made with candle-making wax or beeswax.

Candle-making wax. Crafts stores often carry items produced for candle crafters. For mail-order sources for wax and other candle-making supplies, see the listing on page 156.

Beeswax. The premier and most expensive of the three waxes, beeswax can be more economically bought in bulk; for source listings, see page 156.

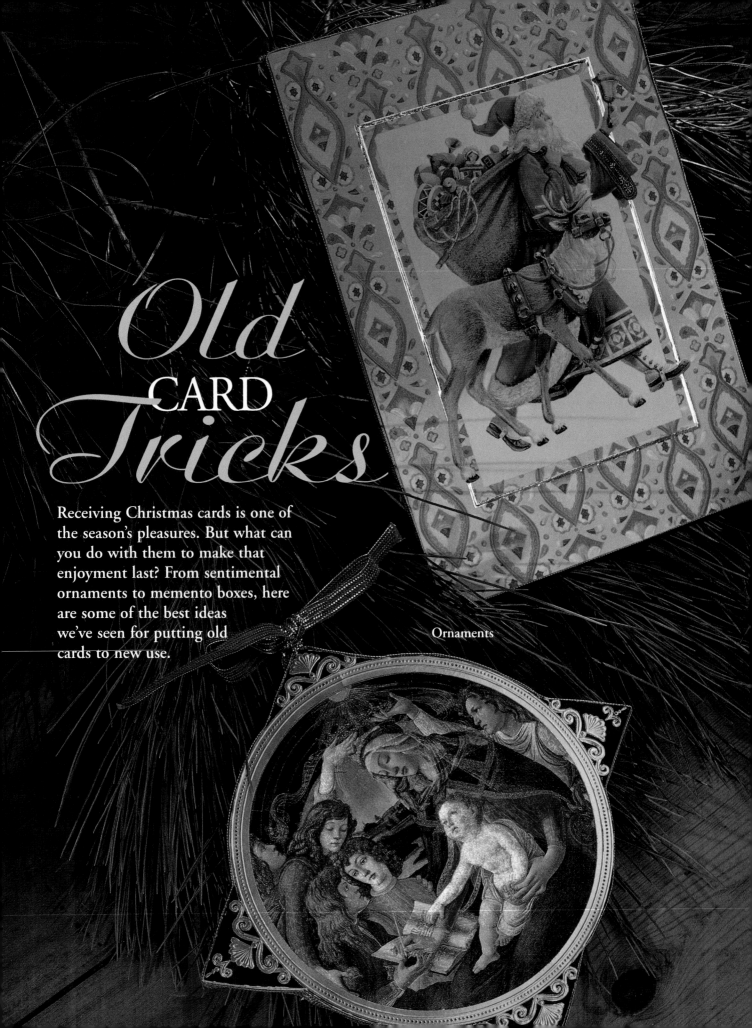

Old CARD Tricks

Receiving Christmas cards is one of the season's pleasures. But what can you do with them to make that enjoyment last? From sentimental ornaments to memento boxes, here are some of the best ideas we've seen for putting old cards to new use.

Ornaments

Ornaments and Package
Toppers *Trim the edges of your ornament or package topper for a dressier look. Consider flat gold braid, plaid ribbon, or jute roping.*

Materials:
Christmas card
Spray adhesive
10" x 10" piece of white foam-core board
Craft knife
¼"-wide gold metallic braid or other trim
Thick craft glue

  1. **Glue card to foam core.** Using scissors, cut card along fold. Using spray adhesive, glue front of card to foam core.
  2. **Cut out ornament.** Using craft knife, cut out ornament. Cut along straight edges of design or, for a more interesting shape, cut out only a portion of the design.
  3. **Trim ornament.** Use craft glue to attach braid to edges of ornament, beginning and ending at top and leaving 6" tails. Knot tails and then tie a bow.

Other Tricks

  • **Half measures.** Cut your cards along the folds and use the front halves as gift tags or postcards.
  • **On the border.** If a card has a decorative border, carefully cut out both the border and the image it surrounds. (A craft knife works best.) Use the border as a mat for a holiday photograph and the center image as a gift tag.
  • **Picture this.** Purchase several miniature picture frames and cut out portions of cards' designs to fit the frames. For hangers, hot-glue loops of red ribbon to the backs.

Package Topper

Keepsake Card Box
Insert a favorite card in the box top; then fill the decorative box with special cards.

Materials:

Deep, sturdy box (see Note below)

Decorative or handmade papers: green, red, ivory, or colors of your choice

Mod Podge glue

1" foam brush

Christmas card

Note: Crafts stores carry papier-mâché boxes, some with two-piece lids that frame cards or photographs. For boxes like the one shown below, see page 156.

1. Prepare paper. Tear paper into pieces of varying sizes and irregular shapes.

2. Cover box. Using foam brush, glue overlapping paper pieces on bottom and lid of box, covering entire surface of each. Let dry.

3. Finish box. If box lid has frame, cut card to fit and insert in frame. Otherwise, trim card to be at least 1" smaller than lid on all sides and glue to top of lid.

More Decoupage Projects
We used Mod Podge for the Keepsake Card Box, but other decoupage glues will work for the following ideas.

• **Scrap sculptures.** Collect a variety of wooden blocks from a construction site or lumberyard. Glue cutouts from old cards to the blocks, covering the blocks completely. Let dry. Group the blocks on a mantel or shelf.

• **Gifted wraps.** Present homemade cookies in tins decoupaged with shapes cut from cards. Giving plants this year? Try decoupaging clay flowerpots. Large pots are ideal for poinsettias. Small pots cleverly conceal tiny treasures—simply stuff the pots with tissue paper and nestle your surprises inside.

Treasure Trunk *During the off-season, the footlocker stores your decorations, but at Christmas it serves as a decoration all on its own.*

Materials:
Footlocker
Assorted Christmas cards
8-ounce container decoupage glue
Foam brushes: 1", 2"

1. **Prepare cards.** Cut out fronts of cards or trim images from cards as desired.

2. **Cover footlocker.** Place cards on footlocker, experimenting with placement to find a pleasing arrangement. Using 1" foam brush, apply glue to backs of cards and replace them on footlocker, brushing away any excess glue. Let dry.

3. **Seal footlocker.** Using 2" foam brush, apply 2 or 3 coats of glue to surface, avoiding metal fasteners and trim. Let dry between applications.

Trunk Tricks *Peggy Williams, the designer who created our decoupaged trunk, has a remarkable eye for detail. These are her tips for turning an inexpensive footlocker into a family heirloom.*

• **Smoothing the edges.** Spread the decoupage glue in thin, even layers on all corners and edges. If the glue is too thick, it will turn white when it dries.

• **Be creative.** Group the card cutouts by color or theme. When Peggy worked on the footlocker shown above, she illustrated Santa's visit on the front. Where the hardware interrupted the flow of images from left to right, she connected them with a narrow band containing a Christmas message.

• **Growing room.** Leave some sides undecorated so you can add cards in future years. Tuck your brushes and decoupage glue inside the trunk so they'll be handy.

• **Others to cover.** Discount stores sell footlockers for $20, but you can also use an old suitcase or trunk. Make sure your glue will work on the material you're covering.

Cluster Bow

Flower Bow

Traditional Bow

KNOW *Bows*

Tying good-looking bows is a useful skill. And with our demonstrations of three favorites, it's easy to learn. Though you may want to add extra for streamers, we tell you how much ribbon our bows require and give tips on making yours smaller or larger.

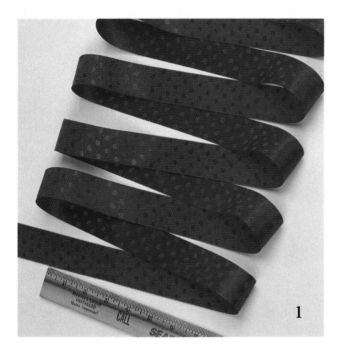

1

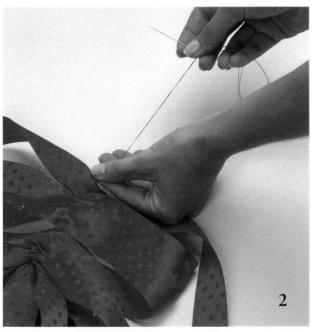

2

Cluster Bow   *This casual bow is simple to scale up or down. To estimate how much ribbon you'll need, multiply the desired diameter of the bow by the desired number of loops—about 8 loops for a small bow, 14 for a medium one, and 20 for a large one. For yardage requirements, divide that total by 36.*

Materials for a 10"-wide bow:
4½ yards 1½"-wide satin double-faced ribbon in
    desired color
Ruler
Masking tape (optional)
Needle
Thread to match ribbon

Note: For ribbon, see sources on page 156.
1. **Loop ribbon.** Using ruler as a guide, fold ribbon into 10"-wide loops arranged side by side as shown, leaving tails at beginning and end. If desired, stabilize outside edges of loops with long lengths of masking tape.
2. **Gather loops.** Thread needle and knot end of thread. Run several large gathering stitches through center of each loop. Remove tape. Pull thread to gather loops, making a bow. Wrap thread around center of bow and knot to secure.

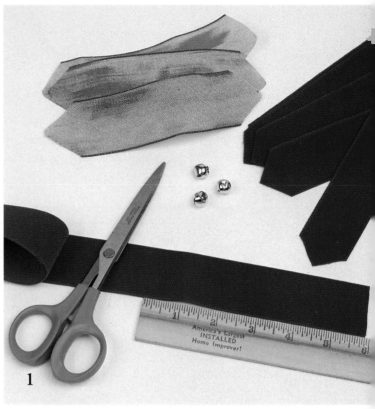

1

Flower Bow
A ribbon flower looks as pretty on a pin or a barrette as it does on a package—all you need to do is hot-glue the bow to a pin back or barrette hardware. To make the bow smaller or larger, just cut the ribbons shorter or longer.

Materials for 6"-wide bow:
1 yard 1½"-wide velvet ribbon in desired color
½ yard 1½"-wide wire-edged ribbon in desired color
½ yard lightweight florist's wire
Ruler
3 (20-mm) gold jingle bells

    1. Cut ribbons and wire. For petals, cut velvet ribbon into 6 (6") lengths. For leaves, cut wire-edged ribbon into 3 (6") lengths. Trim ends to form points.
    Cut wire into 3 (3") lengths and 1 (5") length.
    2. Assemble bow. Using 3" wires, wire petals and leaves together as shown.
    Stack 2 petal sections on top of leaves. String bells onto 5" wire. Centering bells on petals, secure all 3 sections with bell wire, twisting wire ends together at back.

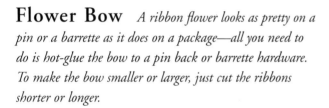

2

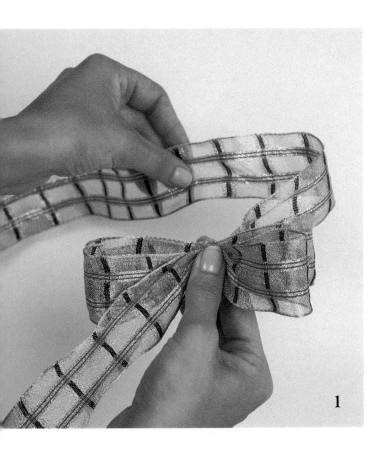

1

2

Traditional Bow

For everything from gifts to wreaths, this bow is the classic choice. Ours is 6" wide and uses 2 yards of ribbon. For larger bows, add ½ yard of ribbon for every 2" increase in size. For smaller bows, subtract ½ yard for every 2" decrease.

Materials for 6"-wide bow:
2 yards 1½"-wide double-faced ribbon in
   desired color
Tape measure
Scrap of florist's wire

   1. Cut and loop ribbon. Cut 1 (18") length of ribbon and set aside.
   Beginning and ending with 6" tails, fold remaining ribbon into 6 (6") loops as shown, pinching ribbon together in center. Wire loops in center to secure.
   2. Finish bow. Loosely knot center of 18" ribbon. Centering knot over wire at center of bow, tie ribbon around wired loops.

Cozy STOCKINGS

Downy fleece and faux lambswool—cheap and easy to sew—make a merry match.

Materials for 1:
Patterns on pages 146–47
Tracing paper
Dressmaker's chalk and pen
½ yard 60"-wide polar fleece in desired color (see
    Note below)
¼ yard imitation lambswool (see Note below)
¼ yard off-white cotton (for cuff lining)
Thread to match fabrics
6" length ¼"-wide flat gold braid

Note: Add ½" seam allowance to stocking and cuff patterns. To order fleece and lambswool, see page 156.

1. **Cut fabrics.** Using tracing paper and dressmaker's chalk, transfer stocking pattern to fleece, and cut 1. Reverse pattern and cut 1 more. Using tracing paper and dressmaker's pen, transfer cuff pattern to lambswool and cotton, and cut 1 from each.

2. **Stitch stocking.** With right sides facing and raw edges aligned, stitch stocking pieces together, leaving top open. Trim seams; do not turn. For hem, baste top edge under ⅝". For hanger, loop braid in half. Insert cut ends under hem at back seam. Fold braid back over hem so that loop extends beyond top of stocking. Topstitch around stocking top, sewing ½" from edge. Turn.

3. **Make cuff.** With right sides facing and raw edges aligned, stitch cuff pieces together, leaving a 2" opening at top. Trim seams, clip curves and corners, and turn. Slipstich opening closed. Referring to photograph, position cuff around top of stocking. Slipstitch cuff in place.

POUND CAKE
Classics

For a versatile collection of recipes, we offer several
delicious versions of this traditional favorite.

Cream Cheese Pound Cake

1½ cups butter, softened
1 (8-ounce) package cream cheese, softened
3 cups sugar
7 large eggs
3 cups all-purpose flour
¼ teaspoon salt
2 teaspoons vanilla extract
Sifted powdered sugar (optional)

Beat butter and cream cheese in a large mixing bowl
at medium speed of an electric mixer about 2 minutes or
until soft and creamy. Gradually add sugar, beating 2
minutes. Add eggs, one at a time, beating just until
yellow disappears after each addition.

Combine flour and salt. Gradually add flour mixture
to butter mixture, beating at low speed just until blended after each addition. Stir in vanilla.

Pour batter into a greased and floured 12-cup Bundt
pan or 10-inch tube pan. Gently swirl a knife through
batter to remove air pockets.

Bake at 325° for 1 hour and 15 minutes or until a
wooden pick inserted in center comes out clean. Cool in
pan on a wire rack 10 to 15 minutes; remove from pan,
and let cool completely on wire rack. Sprinkle with sifted
powdered sugar, if desired. Yield: 1 (10-inch) cake.

Flavorful Variations

Amaretto-Cream Cheese Pound Cake: Add
flour mixture to butter mixture alternately with ½ cup
amaretto or other almond-flavored liqueur, beginning
and ending with flour mixture. Mix at low speed just
until blended after each addition. Omit vanilla extract.
Bake at 325° for 1 hour and 50 minutes or until a
wooden pick inserted in center comes out clean. Cool as
directed. Sprinkle with sifted powdered sugar, if desired.

Chocolate-Cream Cheese Pound Cake:
Reduce sugar to 2½ cups. Melt 4 (1-ounce) squares
semisweet chocolate in a small saucepan over low heat.
Gently stir melted chocolate into batter with vanilla
until thoroughly blended. Bake at 325° for 1 hour and
50 minutes or until a wooden pick inserted in center
comes out clean. Cool as directed. Sprinkle with sifted
powdered sugar, if desired.

Marbled-Cream Cheese Pound Cake: Prepare
batter as directed. Remove 2 cups batter, and stir in 3
tablespoons cocoa until blended. Spoon 2 cups plain batter into prepared pan; top with half of chocolate batter.
Repeat layers, ending with plain batter. Gently swirl batter with a knife to create a marbled effect. Bake at 325°
for 1 hour and 30 minutes or until a wooden pick inserted in center comes out clean. Cool as directed. Sprinkle
with sifted powdered sugar, if desired.

Five Ways to a Great Cake.
Lisa Hooper Talley, who developed these recipes, has tested dozens of pound cakes over the years. She has the following recommendations for baking a perfect pound cake.

1. Indulge. This is one of those happy instances when splurging is actually advisable.

Simply put, premium ingredients make a better cake. That means you should use only real butter (not margarine), premium cream cheese, Grade A large eggs, and real vanilla extract (not imitation flavoring).

Avoid substituting light products for the butter, cream cheese, and eggs. These recipes weren't developed to accommodate low-fat alternatives.

2. Easy does it. When you use your electric mixer, follow the recipe's directions for beating times. Overbeating the ingredients will make the cake tough.

3. Pan prep. Grease and flour every nook and cranny of the inside of your pan, especially if it's a Bundt pan.

Using a pastry brush is an easy way to grease a pan with shortening.

Then coat the shortening with flour. To shake out the excess flour, turn the pan upside down and tap it against the edge of the sink.

4. Best test. The baking time given in a recipe is meant to be used only as a guide. Since oven temperatures vary (sometimes widely), you should rely on the time-honored test: Insert a wooden pick into the cake's center; when it comes out clean, the cake is done.

5. Cooling down. Cool the cake in the pan for 10 to 15 minutes. That's just long enough for the cake to shrink from the pan's sides, but not long enough for it to start sticking to the bottom.

After removing the cake from the pan, place it on a wire rack, which allows heat and moisture to escape from all sides.

Cream Cheese Pound Cake Loaves

1½ cups butter, softened
1 (8-ounce) package cream cheese, softened
3 cups sugar
7 large eggs
3 cups all-purpose flour
¼ teaspoon salt
2 teaspoons vanilla extract

Beat butter and cream cheese in a large mixing bowl at medium speed of an electric mixer about 2 minutes or until soft and creamy. Gradually add sugar, beating 2 minutes. Add eggs, one at a time, beating just until yellow disappears after each addition.

Combine flour and salt. Gradually add flour mixture to butter mixture, beating at low speed just until blended after each addition. Stir in vanilla.

Pour batter into 3 greased and floured 8½- x 4½- x 2½-inch loafpans. Gently swirl a knife through batter to remove air pockets.

Bake at 350° for 45 minutes. Reduce temperature to 300°, and bake 15 to 20 additional minutes or until a wooden pick inserted in center comes out clean. Cool in pans on wire racks 10 to 15 minutes; remove from pans, and cool completely on wire racks. Yield: 3 loaves.

Three Ways to a Great Gift.
For true Christmas presence, consider these wrapping ideas.

1. Wraps in a snap. For speed and elegant simplicity, you can't beat covering a cake in waxed paper or plastic wrap and tying it with a knockout bow.

2. Two gifts in one. Present a cake in its own pan to a kitchenware collector or to someone whose cupboards need stocking. The pan can be brand-new or vintage.

3. Frozen assets. You can freeze pound cakes up to two months. That means you can make them in October and give them away in December.

For a source for the glass ornaments
we used, see page 156.

FROM PLAIN TO
Fancy

Make store-bought ornaments magical. Then hang them on the tree,
give them as gifts, and use them as keepsake party favors.

Star Studded

Decorate the entire surface of
the ornament with self-stick
gold foil stars. (The ones we
used are ⅝" wide.) Repeat the
theme by tying a star-print ribbon bow to the hanger.

Holly Hobbies   Using

tracing paper, trace the holly pattern on page 147. Transfer the
pattern four or five times to
the ornament. Trace over
the pattern lines with craft
glue. Sprinkle gold glit-
ter on the glue. Suspend
the ornament until the
glue dries.

Silver Snowflakes

With a fine-point silver
paint pen, draw four inter-
secting lines to create each
snowflake-like motif. For a
version using different colors,
see the ornament nestled against
the stockings on page 66.

Jewel Zone   Using a clear-

drying craft glue, glue about 20
acrylic gems to the ornament,
placing them randomly. Craft
and fabric stores carry acrylic
gems in many sizes, shapes, and
colors. Small gems—like the 9-mm
ones we used—adhere well to curved surfaces.

Winning Trimmings

First, remove the ornament cap.
Measure from the cap opening,
around the bottom, and back up
to the opening; add 1". Cut
four lengths of ¼" rickrack to
this measurement. Glue the rick-
rack to the ornament, spacing the lengths evenly and
tucking the ends into the opening. Replace the cap.

You Name It   With

a pencil, lightly write the
name and year on the ornament. With a wide-point
paint pen, trace over the pen-
ciled lines and paint polka dots.
This ornament makes a festive
place card or package topper.

TAKE A
Bough

**Floral designer Carole Sullivan has
lots of hints for do-it-yourself decorators,
including how to turn a humble
hanger into a splendid swag.**

Carole is an expert on creating big effects in little time.
At Lagniappe Designs, her company in Birmingham,
Alabama, she plans floral decorations for dozens of
events a year and works with her team to carry them off.
And since Carole also balances work with family, which
includes her husband and five sons, she sets a premium
on the effective use of time and materials.

"At Christmas, when there's so much going on," says
Carole, "I try to make the most of what I already have. I
experiment with whatever's handy, and I often end up
with something more imaginative than what I originally
pictured." Last Christmas she even turned large tomato
cages into towering centerpieces aglow with tiers of
votive candles.

Carole's inventiveness and knack for naturals are two
reasons we asked her for a fresh-picked approach to an
old decorating trick—using a tablecloth hanger as a base
for a greenery swag.

"At the holidays, your front-door decoration gives
guests their first impression of your home, so it pays to
do something creative," says Carole. Her swag, shown in
the photograph at left, sparkles with old Christmas ornaments and colorful holiday ribbon. To learn how she
made it, just turn the page.

Materials for 1 swag:
Tablecloth hanger (available at dry cleaners, often for free)
Boughs of fresh evergreen, such as pine, cedar, Fraser fir, blue spruce, or balsam
21-gauge florist's wire
Wire cutters or snips
Real or artificial berries
Acrylic spray finish (optional)
Artificial fruit
10 or 12 Christmas ornaments
1½ yards each holiday ribbon:
  2"-wide, 1½"-wide
Tacking nail (optional)

1. **Cover hanger with greenery.** Remove cardboard covering. Bend hanger to form upside-down V. Beginning at bottom on 1 side, wire a bough of greenery to bottom, wrap wire to top, and wire a bough to top. Repeat, working toward neck of hanger and continuing to alternate between bottom and top of hanger. At neck of hanger, twist wire and clip.

Repeat to cover remaining side of hanger with greenery.

2. **Add decorative accents.** Wire ornaments to hanger as desired. (We used new ornaments supplemented with antique ornaments from an editor's collection. Look for vintage ornaments at flea markets and antiques shops; reproductions are available at Christmas stores or from the sources listed on page 156.)

If desired, spray fresh berries with acrylic finish to prolong color. Wire on berries and artificial fruit.

3. Finish and hang swag. Weave twisted ribbons into greenery as shown, securing ribbon ends with wire at beginning and end.

To display swag, hang hook of hanger on a door knocker or small nail. For extra stability, wire the hook of hanger to knocker or nail.

Carole's Quick Fixes *Carole is a pro at transforming whatever's on hand into well-turned arrangements and decorations. Here she shares some of her favorite techniques for decorating on the double.*

• **Keep it simple.** Display different containers filled with the same kind of greenery or flowers. Gathering cuttings from one hedgerow or flowerbed is fast, and massing cuttings of a single variety has impact.

• **Add an accent.** Inexpensive ball ornaments can sparkle in a variety of settings. Pile them in a glass bowl and tuck in a few fresh blooms or sprigs of greenery. For a mantel or hearth, wire several pine boughs together at the top and decorate the boughs with several clusters of three ornaments each. Punctuate an evergreen wreath with clusters of silver or gold ornaments, and tie on a big bow of the same color. For a Christmas-tree topiary, hot-glue moss to cover a large Styrofoam cone; using florist's picks, trim the "tree" with miniature ornaments and place it in a concrete or terra-cotta planter.

• **Very berry.** Rangy, berry-laden branches, such as pepper berries or pyracantha berries, look striking in tall, cylindrical vases of varying heights. Half-fill each of the vases with cranberries, arrange the branches in the vases, and pour in just enough water to cover the cranberries.

• **A play on poinsettias.** Rather than displaying poinsettias in their pots, clip the stems bearing large blooms. With the flame from a candle, singe the stems' ends to seal in the milky fluid. Place the sprays in water-filled silver or glass bud vases. For a dramatic look, arrange the vases single file along a mantel, sideboard, or table center.

• **A table that's all set.** For quick napkin rings, roll up each napkin, tie it with ribbon, and tuck in a sprig of greenery and a flower (using whatever is available in your area during the holidays). Place a napkin in the center of each place setting.

• **Name game.** Turn fresh, bright green holly leaves into place cards. Using a silver or gold paint pen, write the name on each leaf and nestle the leaf beside a wine glass or water glass.

German Chocolate Mocha, page 103; Santa napkins, page 80;
Ambrosia Sauce, page 82.

COUNTRY CHRISTMAS PANTRY

This year, treat guests to coffees

laced with Swiss chocolate and

creamy caramel.

Make holiday napkins from

vintage postcards. Or give a few

generous jars of sauces both

savory and sweet.

With our mix of foods and crafts,

you'll have the recipe for creating a

season to remember.

SANTA AT YOUR
Service

He appears on a festive set of cocktail napkins—
each printed with the image from an old copyright-free
postcard. You can use your own cards or the vintage designs
we've reproduced at the back of this book.

Materials:

Color photocopies of vintage postcards on pages
148–49, or color photocopies of other postcards or
greeting cards (see Note below)

100%-cotton fabric, such as muslin or broadcloth

Newsprint

Masking tape

Picture This transfer medium for fabric

Paintbrush

Brayer or round plastic bottle

Paper towels

Metal spoon

Sponge

White paper

Thread to match fabric

Note: This transfer technique reverses original images.
Images on pages 148–49 are already reversed and should
be photocopied as is. If using other postcards or greeting
cards, reverse images on color copier. Before beginning,
wash and press fabric.

1. Prepare materials. On each photocopy, trim away
all white edges. Cut fabric so it is 4" longer and wider
than photocopy. Cover flat work surface with newsprint.
Center fabric on paper. Secure all edges of fabric to
paper with masking tape.

2. Transfer image. Apply approximately 2 tablespoons of transfer medium to front of each image. Using
paintbrush, spread evenly over entire surface.

Lay image facedown on fabric, centering image so
that a 2" border of fabric remains around image. Using
brayer or plastic bottle, press image into fabric, being
careful not to shift image. Remove excess transfer medium from edges with paper towel to prevent discol-
oration of fabric. Continue applying pressure to image
for at least 10 minutes. Use back of spoon to secure corners and edges.

Let fabric dry for 24 hours. Soak fabric in warm
water for 1 hour. Using fingers, carefully rub away paper
to reveal image. Use a sponge in stubborn places. Let
dry. If image is still cloudy, repeat soaking and rubbing
until all paper has been removed.

When dry, lay fabric right side up on ironing board
and cover with white paper. Using iron on hottest setting allowed for type of fabric used, press image for 1
minute to heat-set image onto fabric.

3. Finish napkin. Turn under each raw edge of napkin ⅜" twice, mitering corners. Press. Topstitch hem
close to inner folded edge.

Do not use napkins for 72 hours. Hand-wash in cool
water or machine-wash on gentle cycle. Line-dry, or
tumble-dry on low.

Ambrosia Sauce

Peanut Butter–
Fudge Sauce

Four-Star
SAUCES

With these quick-fix toppings, just mix, pour
or spoon into containers, and enjoy.

Ambrosia Sauce

1½ cups sugar
1 cup pineapple-orange juice
¼ cup butter or margarine
2 teaspoons grated orange rind
4 egg yolks, lightly beaten
½ cup flaked coconut
½ cup chopped pecans, toasted
¼ teaspoon coconut extract
1 (15-ounce) can crushed pineapple, drained
1 (6-ounce) jar red maraschino cherries, chopped

Combine first 5 ingredients in top of a double boiler;
bring water to a boil. Reduce heat to medium-low; cook
15 minutes, stirring constantly. Stir in coconut and
remaining ingredients. Serve warm or chilled over ice
cream, pound cake, or angel food cake. Refrigerate up to
1 week. Yield: 3½ cups.

Peanut Butter–Fudge Sauce

2½ cups firmly packed brown sugar
2½ cups whipping cream
½ cup butter or margarine
2 cups (12 ounces) semisweet chocolate morsels
1 (7-ounce) jar marshmallow cream
½ cup creamy peanut butter
2 teaspoons vanilla extract

Combine first 3 ingredients in a saucepan; bring to a
boil over medium heat. Cook, uncovered, 6 minutes,

stirring occasionally. Cool 2 minutes. Add morsels and remaining ingredients, stirring until morsels melt. Serve warm over ice cream, pound cake, or cheesecake. Refrigerate up to 3 weeks. Yield: 6½ cups.

Roasted Garlic–Parmesan Spread

2 large heads garlic, unpeeled
2 tablespoons olive oil
2 (8-ounce) packages cream cheese, softened
1 cup butter or margarine, softened
1 cup freshly grated Parmesan cheese
1 tablespoon dried Italian seasoning
½ teaspoon freshly ground pepper
1 (4-ounce) jar diced pimiento, drained (optional)

Place garlic on foil; drizzle with oil, and wrap. Bake at 350° for 30 minutes. Cool. Cut off pointed ends of garlic; squeeze pulp from cloves. Beat cream cheese and butter with an electric mixer until creamy. Add pulp, cheese, and remaining ingredients; beat well. Stir in pimiento, if desired. Spread on baguette slices before broiling. Refrigerate up to 2 weeks. Yield: about 4 cups.

Strawberry Syrup

2 (10-ounce) packages frozen strawberries in light
    syrup, thawed
3 cups sugar
1 cup light corn syrup
½ cup orange juice
3 tablespoons strawberry-flavored gelatin
1 teaspoon grated orange rind
¾ teaspoon ground cinnamon

Process strawberries with an electric blender or food processor until smooth. Combine strawberry puree, sugar, and remaining ingredients in a saucepan. Bring to a boil; remove from heat. Serve warm over ice cream or pancakes. Refrigerate up to 3 weeks. Yield: 6 cups.

Roasted Garlic–
Parmesan Spread

Strawberry
Syrup

Crown Roast of Pork with Cranberry–Wild Rice Stuffing

Dinner
FOR SIX,
SIMPLY
Divine

Spiced Pear and Pecan Salad

Crown Roast of Pork with
Cranberry–Wild Rice Stuffing

Green Beans with
Balsamic-Glazed Onions

Pepper-Parmesan Country Bread

Chocolate-Raspberry Roulage

Serves 6

This menu received rave reviews in our Test Kitchens, and we predict your guests will love it, too. What *you'll* love are two qualities we've built into the plan.

TIME-SAVERS. Every recipe except the entrée features two preparation options. Use the from-scratch version when you want to go all out. Or try our shortcut suggestion, found at the end of each recipe, when time is of the essence.

FLEXIBILITY. If hosting a special dinner during the busy holiday season doesn't seem realistic, choose a time that does—perhaps an evening before Thanksgiving or after New Year's. In these dishes, traditional ingredients such as cranberries and pumpkin pie spice are subtle influences. And crown roast of pork isn't quite the Christmas classic that turkey or ham is. The result is a festive menu that works well all winter long.

Spiced Pear
and Pecan Salad

Spiced Pear and Pecan Salad

⅓ cup plus 2 tablespoons olive oil, divided
¼ cup sugar
¾ teaspoon salt
1½ teaspoons pumpkin pie spice
1⅓ cups pecan halves
1½ cups apple cider
3 shallots, minced
2 tablespoons honey mustard
¼ teaspoon pumpkin pie spice
8 cups torn mixed baby greens
2 medium-size firm ripe pears
4 ounces crumbled blue cheese

Combine 2 tablespoons oil, sugar, salt, and 1½ teaspoons pumpkin pie spice; add pecans, tossing to coat. Spread pecans in a single layer in a 15- x 10- x 1-inch jellyroll pan. Bake at 350° for 18 to 20 minutes or until toasted, stirring occasionally. Spread pecans in a single layer on paper towels to drain; let cool completely.

Combine cider and shallots in a small saucepan; bring to a boil. Boil 20 minutes or until mixture is reduced to ½ cup. Add remaining ⅓ cup oil, honey mustard, and ¼ teaspoon pumpkin pie spice, stirring with a wire whisk until blended. Set aside, and keep warm.

Divide greens evenly among six individual salad plates. Core pears, and cut in half lengthwise. Cut pear halves lengthwise into ¼-inch slices. Top greens evenly with pear slices and pecans; sprinkle evenly with blue cheese. Drizzle warm dressing evenly over salads. Serve immediately. Yield: 6 servings.

QUICK TIP. Substitute commercial honey roasted pecans for the prepared pecans, and ¾ cup commercial honey mustard salad dressing for the prepared dressing.

Crown Roast of Pork with Cranberry–Wild Rice Stuffing

1 (6-ounce) package wild rice
¾ pound mild Italian link sausage, casings removed
1 cup chopped purple onion
2 tablespoons minced garlic
1 tablespoon olive oil
2 (3-ounce) packages dried cranberries (1 cup)
1 cup chopped fresh parsley
2 tablespoons minced fresh thyme
2 tablespoons grated orange rind
½ teaspoon salt
1½ teaspoons freshly ground pepper, divided
8 sprigs fresh thyme, divided
1 (5-pound) crown roast of pork (10 to 12 chops)
1 cup Madeira
Garnishes: fresh cranberries, fresh thyme sprigs

Cook rice according to package directions; drain.

Brown sausage in a large skillet, stirring until it crumbles; drain and set aside.

Cook onion and garlic in hot oil in a large skillet over medium-high heat, stirring constantly, until tender.

Combine rice, sausage, onion mixture, dried cranberries, parsley, minced thyme, orange rind, salt, and ½ teaspoon pepper. Reserve and set aside 1½ cups rice mixture. Spoon remaining rice mixture into a greased 11- x 7- x 1½-inch baking dish; top with 6 thyme sprigs. Set aside.

Sprinkle roast with remaining 1 teaspoon pepper. Place roast, bone ends up, on a rack in a greased shallow roasting pan. Insert meat thermometer, making sure it does not touch bone or fat. Spoon reserved 1½ cups rice mixture into roast. Place remaining 2 thyme sprigs on rice mixture. Bake at 350° for 1½ hours or until thermometer registers 160°, basting with Madeira.

Place dish of rice mixture in oven 20 minutes before roast is done, and bake until thoroughly heated.

Cover roast loosely with foil; let stand 10 minutes before carving. Transfer to a serving platter; garnish, if desired. Slice between ribs to serve. Serve with rice mixture. Yield: 6 servings.

Green Beans with Balsamic-Glazed Onions

¼ cup plus 2 tablespoons honey
¼ cup balsamic vinegar
¼ cup olive oil
½ teaspoon salt
½ teaspoon freshly ground pepper
1 (16-ounce) package frozen pearl onions,
    thawed and drained
1½ pounds fresh green beans

Combine half each of first 5 ingredients; add onions, tossing gently to coat. Spread onion mixture in a lightly greased 15- x 10- x 1-inch jellyroll pan. Bake at 400° for 20 minutes or until onions are tender and glazed, stirring occasionally.

Wash beans; trim ends, and remove strings. Cut beans in half crosswise. Cook beans in boiling salted water to cover 10 minutes or until tender; drain.

Combine remaining half of first 5 ingredients in a large bowl; add onions and beans, tossing gently to coat. Serve immediately. Yield: 6 servings.

QUICK TIP. Substitute 1 (16-ounce) package frozen cut green beans, cooked according to package directions and drained, for fresh green beans.

Pepper-Parmesan Country Bread

1 package active dry yeast
1 cup warm water (105° to 115°)
1 cup warm milk (105° to 115°)
1 cup freshly grated Parmesan cheese
⅔ cup chopped onion
⅔ cup chopped canned roasted red peppers
½ cup yellow cornmeal
2 tablespoons sugar
2 tablespoons olive oil
2 teaspoons salt
2 teaspoons cracked pepper
3 to 3½ cups unbleached all-purpose flour
2 cups whole wheat flour
2 tablespoons yellow cornmeal

Combine first 3 ingredients in a 2-cup liquid measuring cup; let stand 5 minutes.

Combine yeast mixture, Parmesan cheese, and next 7 ingredients in a large mixing bowl; beat at medium speed of an electric mixer until well blended. Add 2 cups all-purpose flour and whole wheat flour; beat well. Gradually stir in enough remaining all-purpose flour to make a soft dough.

Turn dough out onto a well-floured surface; knead until smooth and elastic (about 5 minutes). Place in a greased bowl; turn to grease top. Cover and let rise in a warm place (85°), 1 hour or until doubled in bulk.

Sprinkle 2 tablespoons cornmeal on a large baking sheet; set aside.

Punch dough down, and divide in half. Shape each half of dough into a round loaf; place loaves on prepared baking sheet. Cover and let rise in a warm place (85°), free from drafts, 25 minutes or until doubled in bulk.

Bake at 350° for 40 to 45 minutes or until loaves sound hollow when tapped. Remove loaves from baking sheet; let cool on wire racks. Yield: 2 loaves.

QUICK TIP. If you don't have time to prepare this recipe, purchase hearty round loaves of bread from a bakery, and serve them instead.

Crown Roast of Pork with Cranberry–Wild Rice Stuffing, Pepper-Parmesan
Country Bread, and Green Beans with Balsamic-Glazed Onions

Chocolate-Raspberry Roulage

Chocolate-Raspberry Roulage

½ cup plus 2 tablespoons cocoa, divided
¼ cup all-purpose flour
4 large eggs, separated
¼ teaspoon salt
½ cup plus 1 tablespoon sugar, divided
¼ cup plus 2 tablespoons seedless raspberry jam,
    melted and divided
¾ cup whipping cream, divided
4 ounces premium-quality white chocolate, chopped
Raspberry Sauce
Garnish: fresh mint sprigs

Grease a 15- x 10- x 1-inch jellyroll pan. Line with wax paper; grease wax paper. Flour wax paper and sides of pan. Set aside.

Sift together ½ cup cocoa and flour; set aside.

Beat egg whites and salt at high speed of an electric mixer until foamy; gradually add ¼ cup plus 2 tablespoons sugar, 1 tablespoon at a time, beating until stiff peaks form and sugar dissolves (2 to 4 minutes). Set aside.

Combine remaining 3 tablespoons sugar, egg yolks, and 2 tablespoons jam in a large bowl; stir well with a wire whisk. Fold in beaten egg whites. Gently fold in cocoa mixture until blended. Spread mixture evenly in prepared pan. Bake at 350° for 15 minutes.

Sift remaining 2 tablespoons cocoa in a 15- x 10-inch rectangle on a cloth towel. When cake is done, immediately loosen from sides of pan, and turn out onto prepared towel. Peel off wax paper. Starting at narrow end, roll up cake and towel together; let cool completely on a wire rack, seam side down.

Combine ¼ cup whipping cream and white chocolate in a small saucepan; cook over low heat, stirring constantly, until chocolate melts. Cool completely.

Beat remaining ½ cup whipping cream in a large bowl at high speed of an electric mixer until frothy. Gradually add cooled white chocolate mixture to whipping cream; beat until thick and smooth. (Mixture may appear curdled, but will smooth as beating continues.)

Unroll cake, and remove towel. Brush remaining ¼ cup melted jam over cake; spread white chocolate mixture over jam. Carefully reroll cake without towel; place, seam side down, on a serving plate. Cover and chill at least 1 hour before serving.

Spoon 2 tablespoons Raspberry Sauce onto each dessert plate. Cut roulage into 1-inch slices; place 1 slice on each plate. Garnish, if desired. Serve immediately with remaining Raspberry Sauce. Yield: 8 servings.

Raspberry Sauce

2 (10-ounce) packages frozen raspberrries in light
    syrup, thawed
3 tablespoons cornstarch
2 teaspoons sugar
3 tablespoons Chambord or other raspberry-flavored
    liqueur
2 tablespoons lemon juice

Place raspberries in container of an electric blender or food processor; cover and process until smooth. Pour mixture through a wire-mesh strainer into a small heavy saucepan; discard seeds. Add cornstarch and sugar to strained mixture, stirring until smooth.

Cook over low heat, stirring constantly, until mixture is thickened. Remove from heat, and stir in liqueur and lemon juice. Cover and chill thoroughly. Stir before serving. Yield: 2 cups.

QUICK TIP. Instead of baking a roulage from scratch, buy one from a bakery, and then prepare the Raspberry Sauce to serve with the purchased roulage.

A *Glass* ACT

Add some sparkle to your holiday table with hand-painted champagne flutes and dessert plates.

Materials for 6 flutes and 6 plates:
Pattern on page 149
6 clear glass flutes
6 (7") clear glass plates
Tracing paper
Pop-up sponge
Paper plates
Acrylic enamel paints: metallic gold, silver
2"-wide drafting tape

1. **Wash items.** Wash flutes and plates in warm, sudsy water; rinse and dry thoroughly. Set plates aside.

2. **Paint flutes.** Using tracing paper, transfer star pattern to sponge. Cut out. Dip sponge in water to expand. Wring out water; let dry. Squeeze gold paint onto a paper plate. Dab sponge in paint; blot to remove excess. Sponge-paint stars on outside of each flute, leaving rim unpainted. Sponge-paint 1 star on each stem foot.

3. **Paint plates.** Cut 2 (1") squares from sponge. Dip sponge in water to expand. Wring out water; let dry. For each plate, cut 5 or 6 strips of tape equal to diameter of plate. Tear each strip in half lengthwise, creating uneven edges. Place plate right side down on work surface.

Apply 5 or 6 tape strips vertically to back of plate (see Diagram).

Squeeze gold and silver paints onto separate paper plates. Dab 1 sponge in 1 color of paint; blot excess. Sponge-paint stripes on untaped glass, alternating colors. Let dry. Remove tape. Apply new strips of tape horizontally to form checkerboard. Repeat sponging. Remove tape promptly. (Some paint may peel when removing second row of tape.) Let dry; then touch up. Following manufacturer's instructions, allow paint to cure; then heat-set in oven as directed.

Diagram

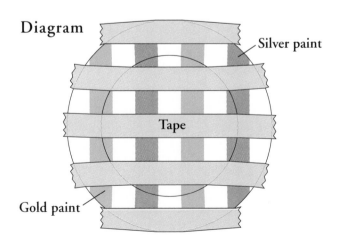

Silver paint

Tape

Gold paint

Wrap UP CHRISTMAS Cheer

To give a certain distinction to wine or another store-bought gift, present it in a velvet bag.

Materials for 1 bag:
½ yard 40"-wide velvet or other festive fabric (see Note below)
Thread to match fabric
¾ yard satin cording with tassels

Note: All seam allowances are ½". For velvet we used, see source listing on page 156.

1. Sew bag. From velvet, cut 2 (7" x 23") pieces. With right sides facing and raw edges aligned, stitch pieces together along 3 sides, leaving 1 short end open for top.

2. Finish bag. For top hem, turn under ⅝" and stitch ½" from folded edge. Trim seams, clip corners, and turn right side out. Fold 4"–5" of top edge to inside of bag.

3. Wrap gift. Insert bottle, adjust top edge of bag as needed, and tie cording around neck of bottle to secure.

The More, the Merrier *While you're making holiday bags, stitch up a few more from different fabrics and get a jump on next year's special occasions.*

• **Kitchen aids.** Dress up flavored oils or vinegars with red-and-white checked fabric tied with raffia.

• **Splendor in the bath.** Present bath oils in bags of linen or brocade. Tie with satin ribbons.

• **Seasonable greetings.** In winter, tuck a merlot or cabernet into a flannel bag tied with twine. In summer, slip a chablis or chardonnay into a bag made of sheer fabric and top it with a tulle bow.

NINE TOUGH
Cookies

Box, bag, or even mail these sturdy sweets. They can take it—
all while looking and tasting terrific.

Chunky Chocolate Cookies

1 cup butter or margarine, softened
1 cup sugar
1 cup firmly packed dark brown sugar
2 large eggs
2 teaspoons vanilla extract
3 cups all-purpose flour
½ teaspoon baking soda
½ teaspoon salt
½ cup cocoa
1 (10-ounce) package semisweet chocolate chunks
1 cup coarsely chopped walnuts

   Beat butter with an electric mixer until creamy; add sugars, beating well. Add eggs and vanilla; beat well.
   Combine flour, baking soda, salt, and cocoa; add to butter mixture, beating well. Stir in chocolate chunks and walnuts.
   Drop dough by rounded tablespoonfuls 2 inches apart onto lightly greased cookie sheets.
   Bake at 350° for 10 minutes. Cool 1 minute on cookie sheets; cool completely on wire racks. Yield: 4½ dozen.

Vanilla-Cherry Cookies

1 (6-ounce) jar red maraschino cherries, drained
1 (6-ounce) jar green maraschino cherries, drained
½ cup butter or margarine, softened
½ cup shortening
1 (3-ounce) package cream cheese, softened
1 cup sugar
1 cup firmly packed brown sugar
2 large eggs
1½ teaspoons vanilla extract
2 cups all-purpose flour
1 teaspoon baking powder
½ teaspoon salt
1 cup quick-cooking oats, uncooked
1 cup crisp rice cereal
1 cup chopped pecans
1 cup flaked coconut
1 (10-ounce) package vanilla-flavored morsels

   Chop cherries; drain on paper towels. Set aside.
   Beat butter, shortening, and cream cheese with an electric mixer until creamy; add sugars, beating well. Add eggs and vanilla; beat well.
   Combine flour, baking powder, and salt; add to butter mixture, beating well. Stir in cherries, oats, and remaining ingredients.
   Drop dough by rounded tablespoonfuls 2 inches apart onto lightly greased cookie sheets.
   Bake at 350° for 12 minutes. Cool 1 minute on cookie sheets; cool completely on wire racks. Yield: about 4 dozen.

Honey Roasted
Peanut Cookies

Chunky Chocolate
Cookies

Vanilla-Cherry
Cookies

Honey Roasted Peanut Cookies

¾ cup butter or margarine, softened

¾ cup creamy peanut butter

1 cup firmly packed brown sugar

½ cup honey

2 large eggs

1 teaspoon vanilla extract

2½ cups all-purpose flour

1 teaspoon baking soda

½ teaspoon salt

1¼ cups chopped honey roasted peanuts

Beat butter and peanut butter with an electric mixer until creamy; add brown sugar and honey, beating well. Add eggs and vanilla; beat well.

Combine flour, baking soda, and salt; add to butter mixture, beating well. Stir in peanuts. Cover and chill at least 2 hours.

Shape chilled dough into 1-inch balls; place balls 2 inches apart on lightly greased cookie sheets. Flatten balls in a crisscross pattern with a fork dipped in flour.

Bake at 350° for 8 minutes. Cool 1 minute on cookie sheets; cool completely on wire racks. Yield: 6½ dozen.

Chocolate–Peanut
Butter Swirls

Butterscotch
Blondies

Spiced Apple–Oatmeal Cookies

Butterscotch Blondies

2 cups (12 ounces) butterscotch morsels, divided
½ cup butter or margarine
1 cup firmly packed brown sugar
½ cup sugar
2 large eggs
1½ teaspoons vanilla extract
1¾ cups all-purpose flour
1½ teaspoons baking powder
½ teaspoon salt
1 (7.5-ounce) package almond brickle chips
¾ cup chopped pecans

Combine ½ cup butterscotch morsels and butter in a saucepan; cook over low heat until melted, stirring often. Cool 5 minutes.

Beat sugars, eggs, and vanilla with an electric mixer until blended. Add butterscotch mixture; beat well.

Combine flour, baking powder, and salt; add to sugar mixture, beating just until blended.

Stir 1 cup butterscotch morsels and brickle chips into batter. Pour batter into a lightly greased 13- x 9- x 2-inch pan. Sprinkle batter with remaining ½ cup butterscotch morsels and chopped pecans. Bake at 350° for 30 minutes. Cool completely in pan; cut into bars. Yield: 2½ dozen.

Chocolate–Peanut Butter Swirls

¾ cup butter or margarine, softened
1¼ cups firmly packed dark brown sugar
1 large egg
2 tablespoons milk
1½ teaspoons vanilla extract
3 cups all-purpose flour
1 teaspoon baking powder
¼ teaspoon salt
2 (1-ounce) squares semisweet chocolate, melted
¼ cup plus 2 tablespoons creamy peanut butter

Beat butter with an electric mixer until creamy; add sugar, beating well. Add egg, milk, and vanilla; beat well.

Combine flour, baking powder, and salt; add to butter mixture, beating well.

Divide dough in half. Stir chocolate into one portion of dough; shape into a ball. Stir peanut butter into remaining portion of dough; shape into a ball.

Roll each portion of dough between two sheets of wax paper into a 14- x 8-inch rectangle. Remove top sheets of wax paper. Invert peanut butter dough onto chocolate dough; peel off wax paper, and press doughs together lightly with a rolling pin. Roll up dough, starting at long side, peeling wax paper from dough while rolling. Wrap roll in wax paper; chill at least 2 hours.

Cut roll into ¼-inch slices; place 2 inches apart on lightly greased cookie sheets. Bake at 350° for 10 minutes. Cool 1 minute on cookie sheets; cool completely on wire racks. Yield: 4½ dozen.

Spiced Apple–Oatmeal Cookies

¼ cup butter or margarine, softened
½ cup shortening
1¼ cups firmly packed dark brown sugar
¾ cup sugar
2 large eggs
1¼ cups cinnamon applesauce
1½ teaspoons vanilla extract
1½ cups all-purpose flour
1 teaspoon baking soda
½ teaspoon salt
2 teaspoons ground cinnamon
½ teaspoon ground nutmeg
¼ teaspoon ground cloves
3 cups quick-cooking oats, uncooked
1 cup chopped dried apple
1 cup raisins

Beat butter and shortening with an electric mixer until creamy; add sugars, beating well. Add eggs, applesauce, and vanilla; beat well.

Combine flour and next 5 ingredients; add to butter mixture, beating well. Stir in oats, apple, and raisins.

Drop dough by tablespoonfuls 2 inches apart onto ungreased cookie sheets. Bake at 350° for 12 minutes. Cool 1 minute on cookie sheets; cool completely on wire racks. Yield: 4 dozen.

White Chocolate–Almond Gems

¾ cup butter or margarine, softened
4 (1-ounce) squares white chocolate, melted and
  cooled
¾ cup sugar
¾ cup firmly packed brown sugar
1 large egg
¼ cup milk
1 teaspoon vanilla extract
¼ teaspoon almond extract
2¼ cups all-purpose flour
1 teaspoon baking powder
¼ teaspoon salt
2¼ cups finely chopped natural almonds, divided
36 white chocolate and milk chocolate kisses
36 milk chocolate kisses with almonds

Beat butter and white chocolate with an electric
mixer until creamy; add sugars, beating well. Add egg
and next 3 ingredients; beat well. Combine flour, baking
powder, and salt; add to butter mixture, beating well.
Stir in ½ cup almonds. Cover and chill at least 1 hour.

Shape dough into 1-inch balls; roll in remaining
almonds. Place 2 inches apart on lightly greased cookie
sheets. Bake at 375° for 8 minutes. Unwrap kisses, and
press 1 kiss into top of each cookie; bake 2 additional
minutes. Cool 1 minute on cookie sheets; cool completely on wire racks. Yield: 4½ dozen.

Turtle Cheesecake Brownies

1 cup butter or margarine
4 (1-ounce) squares unsweetened chocolate
2¼ cups sugar
4 large eggs, lightly beaten
2 teaspoons vanilla extract
¼ teaspoon salt
1¼ cups all-purpose flour, divided
1 cup coarsely chopped pecans
2 (3-ounce) packages cream cheese, softened
2 large eggs
1 (12-ounce) jar caramel topping

Melt butter and chocolate in a large saucepan over
low heat; remove pan from heat.

Stir in sugar, 4 eggs, vanilla, salt, 1 cup plus 2 tablespoons flour, and pecans, stirring until blended after
each addition. Pour half of batter into a lightly greased
13- x 9- x 2-inch baking pan; reserve remaining chocolate batter.

Beat cream cheese at medium speed of an electric
mixer until creamy. Add remaining 2 tablespoons flour,
2 eggs, and caramel topping; beat until smooth. Pour
evenly over chocolate batter.

Drop reserved chocolate batter by ¼ cupfuls over
cream cheese batter; swirl batter with a knife to create a
marbled effect. Bake at 350° for 42 minutes. Cool in
pan; cut into bars. Yield: 2 dozen.

Chips Galore Cookies

1 cup butter or margarine, softened
1 cup sugar
1 cup firmly packed brown sugar
2 large eggs
1 teaspoon vanilla extract
2½ cups all-purpose flour
1 teaspoon baking soda
½ teaspoon salt
1 cup chopped pecans
½ cup vanilla-flavored morsels
½ cup butterscotch-flavored morsels
½ cup peanut butter-flavored morsels
½ cup semisweet chocolate morsels

Beat butter with an electric mixer until creamy; add sugars, beating well. Add eggs and vanilla; beat well.

Combine flour, baking soda, and salt; add to butter mixture, beating well. Stir in pecans and remaining ingredients.

Drop dough by rounded tablespoonfuls 2 inches apart on lightly greased cookie sheets. Bake at 350° for 15 minutes. Cool 1 minute on cookie sheets; cool completely on wire racks. Yield: 4 dozen.

Chips Galore Cookies

Turtle Cheesecake Brownies

White Chocolate–Almond Gems

COFFEES TO *Carol* ABOUT

Rich, creamy, and fragrant with spices, each of these coffees gets its character from only a few ingredients.

Cinnamon-Pecan Coffee

Cinnamon-Pecan Coffee—To prepare the cinnamon syrup, combine 1 cup sugar and 4 (3-inch) cinnamon sticks, broken, in the container of an electric blender or food processor; cover and process until cinnamon is finely minced. Combine sugar mixture and ½ cup water in a saucepan; bring to a boil, stirring constantly. Reduce heat, and cook 1 minute, stirring constantly. Cool completely. Pour liquid through a wire-mesh strainer into a glass jar; discard cinnamon.

   Hot Version: For each serving, combine ¾ cup hot brewed Southern pecan–flavored coffee, 1 tablespoon cinnamon syrup, and 1 teaspoon brown sugar in a mug. Stir in half-and-half, garnish with whipped cream, and sprinkle with ground cinnamon, if desired.

   Iced Version: For each serving, combine ¾ cup cold brewed Southern pecan-flavored coffee, 1 tablespoon cinnamon syrup, and 1 teaspoon brown sugar in a tall glass; stir in ½ cup half-and-half or milk. Add ice. Serve with a cinnamon stick stirrer, if desired.

Toffee Coffee—For each serving, combine ¾ cup hot brewed Swiss chocolate-almond coffee, 2 teaspoons butterscotch topping, 2 teaspoons chocolate syrup, and ⅛ teaspoon almond extract in a mug. Top with sweetened whipped cream, and sprinkle with chopped English toffee-flavored candy bars, if desired.

German Chocolate Mocha—Combine 4 cups hot brewed coffee, 3 tablespoons caramel topping, 3 tablespoons chocolate syrup, and 1 teaspoon coconut extract; pour mixture into 4 mugs. Add half-and-half or milk, if desired. Top with small scoops of fudge ripple ice cream. Garnish with maraschino cherries, if desired. Makes 4 servings.

Toffee Coffee

German Chocolate Mocha

SHE SETS HER TABLE *By Design*

Angèle Parlange, a New Orleans designer, borrows from past and present to create such appealing pieces as these table decorations.

It's not surprising that Angèle mixes fleurs-de-lis and French script with the crowns of Mardi Gras. For this creative woman, blending old and new is a way of life.

Angèle spent her childhood in New Roads, Louisiana, in a plantation home built by ancestors in the 1750s. Says Angèle, "Even now, a great source of inspiration is my family legacy, especially the European traditions passed on by my grandmother Parlange."

After moving to New Orleans, Angèle began designing smart party dresses for friends and then accents for the home. Her throw pillows—which sported belts and other fashionable notions—were so popular that she started a line of home accessories. Today Angèle Parlange Design, her Uptown shop, boasts her furniture, hand-painted linens, and other creations. And her work has attracted the attention of magazines like *Vogue, Bon Appétit,* and *Southern Accents.*

As friends attest, Angèle's flair also extends to entertaining. That's especially true at Christmas, when she likes to use common materials for creating uncommon effects. A fine example in the tablescape shown here is the rosemary candle pots that serve as both centerpiece and party favor. To learn how to make these and the other elements, keep reading.

"It's fun to take a traditional symbol— like a *star* or a *crown*—and make it seem brand-new."

Invitations *Guests will know something special is in store when you send them one-of-a kind cards.*

Materials for 1:
Pattern on page 150
Tracing paper
8" x 10½" piece of apple green matboard
   or card stock
Red construction paper
Craft knife
Black permanent marker
Gold metallic paint and paintbrush
Spray adhesive
4 or 5 star-shaped acrylic gems or rhinestones
Hot-glue gun and glue sticks

Note: For a source for acrylic gems and rhinestones, see page 156.

1. **Cut out crown and band.** Using tracing paper, transfer crown to matboard and band to paper. Cut out crown with craft knife. Cut out band with scissors. Using marker, write invitation on band; set aside.

2. **Paint crown.** Using gold paint, outline points of crown and paint ends. Paint bottom third of crown. Let dry. Paint sides and back of crown. Let dry.

3. **Attach band.** Referring to photograph, use spray adhesive to attach band.

4. **Attach acrylic gems.** Referring to photograph, hot-glue gems to crown below band.

Place Cards *Make these coordinating place markers in the shapes of stars and crowns, or enlarge them to make a set that doubles as coasters.*

Materials for 1:
Patterns on page 151
Tracing paper
5" x 7" piece of apple green matboard
Craft knife
Gold metallic paint and paintbrush
5 or 6 (9-mm) red acrylic gems or rhinestones
Hot-glue gun and glue sticks
Black permanent marker
Long fireplace matchstick for stand (optional)
For coasters: 8"-square matboard, black paint pen,
   clear acrylic spray sealer

Note: For Angèle's gold-leaf resin coasters, see source listing on page 156.

1. **Cut out place card.** Using tracing paper, transfer desired pattern to matboard. Cut out with craft knife.

2. **Paint place card.** Using gold paint, paint all points. Let dry. Paint sides and back. Let dry.

3. **Attach acrylic gems and write name.** Glue gems to place card. Using marker, write name on place card.

4. **Make stand.** Cut matchstick into 2 (2"-long) pieces. Trim both ends of sticks at opposing 45° angles. Paint sticks gold. Let dry. Glue sticks together forming a V. Glue wide end of V to back of place card.

5. **Make coaster/place card.** Enlarge pattern as indicated. Transfer to matboard and cut out. Paint gold and let dry. Write name in center with paint pen. Spray with several coats of sealer. Let dry.

Napkin Wraps
To dress up plain white napkins, stack a velvet square on each one and slip both through a napkin ring.

Materials for 1:
⅝ yard 40"-wide ruby velvet with
   festive print (see Note below)
¼ yard 45"-wide burlap
Thread to match burlap
Napkin ring

Note: Finished size of napkin wrap is 20" square. For a source for hand-printed velvet, see page 156.

1. Cut out fabrics. Cut 1 (20") square from velvet. For binding, cut 4 (2½" x 20½") strips from burlap.

2. Bind edges of velvet. Turn under ¼" on long edges of burlap and press. Then fold binding in half lengthwise and press. Pin 1 folded binding strip to 1 edge of velvet, sandwiching raw edges of velvet inside. Topstitch close to inner edge of burlap, turning ends under. Repeat to bind remaining edges.

3. Fold napkin. Referring to photograph, tuck napkin inside velvet wrap and secure with napkin ring.

Rosemary Candle Pots
Rosemary, the herb of remembrance, makes a meaningful party favor. Group the pots in the table's center for a fragrant focus, and later give them to your guests.

Materials for 1 pot:
3" terra-cotta pot
1"-wide masking tape (optional)
Metallic paints: red, green
Paintbrushes
3 or 4 star-shaped acrylic gems
Hot-glue gun and glue sticks
Foil for lining
3" square of florist's foam
1½" x 6" decorative candle
Sprigs of fresh rosemary
Decorative moss

Note: For sources for acrylic gems and hand-rolled candles, see page 156.

1. Decorate pot. For vertical stripes, cut tape into 6 (4"-long) strips and place them evenly around pot. Paint untaped areas red. Let dry. Remove tape. Paint remaining areas green. Let dry. Glue acrylic gems to pot as desired.

2. Prepare pot. Line bottom of pot with foil. Place pot upside down on top of foam. Press pot through foam, filling pot. Saturate foam with water; leave to drain. Press candle into center of foam until secure. Insert rosemary sprigs around candle. Tightly pack top of pot with moss.

3. Assemble centerpiece. Gather cake stands and plates of varying heights, fresh artichokes, grapes, and dried pomegranates. Stack cake stands and arrange plates around them. Referring to photograph on facing page, arrange pots, fruits and vegetables as shown.

PLEASURES OF THE SEASON

For the little ones on your
Christmas list, decorate
toasty toboggans and create a
warming memory.
Then let the talented women
known as Kindred Spirits show
you how to design your own
country charm.
And for the quickest gifts of all,
follow our tips for packaging
festive fruits—
to wrap up the season with flair.

PHOTO ALBUM
Alchemy

Weave three colors of ribbons into checkerboard covers and transform dime-store photo albums into colorful treasures. For special occasion albums, simply vary your palette—choose pastels for a wedding or cheery hues for a birthday or Christmas.

For a source for satin ribbon and photo books, see page 156.

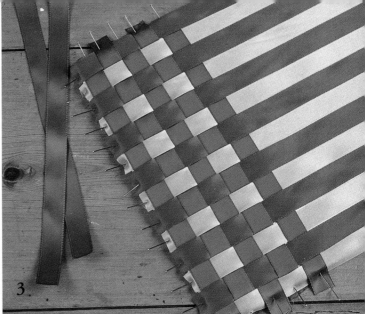

1. **Cut out base.** For a hardcover photo album for either 3½" x 5¼" or 4" x 6" photographs, you will need to make a woven-ribbon cover measuring 9" x 14". Cover will require 3 colors of ⅝"-wide double-faced satin ribbon: 2⅞ yards each of first 2 colors and 5⅞ yards of third color. To make a base to weave ribbons on, use ruler and pencil to mark 9" x 14" rectangle on large piece of foam-core board. Using craft knife and ruler, cut out base along marked lines. Also cut a 9" x 14" piece of lightweight fusible interfacing; set aside.

2. **Begin weaving.** From first 2 colors, cut 7 (14½") strips each. From third color, cut 22 (9½") strips. Pin ends of first 2 colors of ribbons to short ends of foam core, alternating colors. Beginning at corner of 1 long end, weave 1 length of third color under and over horizontal ribbons, pinning ribbon ends to secure. Then weave second length of third color, weaving under and over alternate horizontal ribbons. Pin ends.

3. **Finish weaving.** Continue weaving lengths of third color in this manner until foam core is completely covered. Adjust ribbons so that they are as tightly woven as possible, removing and reinserting pins as necessary. Then adjust pins and ribbons so that pins are parallel to tabletop and so that ribbons are taut. Following manufacturer's instructions, use an iron to fuse 9" x 14" piece of lightweight interfacing to woven ribbons. Remove pins.

4. **Cover album.** Center opened album on wrong side of woven ribbons. Hot-glue album front to ribbons; let dry. Repeat to glue spine and then back to ribbons. Trim ribbons ¾" outside all edges of cover. Wrap corners to inside; glue. Then wrap top, side, and bottom edges to inside; glue. For ties, cut 2 (13½") lengths of ribbon. Glue end of 1 length each to inside of front cover and back cover. From ¼ yard of fabric, cut 2 lining pieces to fit inside front and back covers, and glue in place.

Reindeer

Pal

Children can't resist this gangly, goggle-eyed reindeer—
and frankly we can't, either. Making the stuffed deer is
easy when you take it one hoof at a time.

Materials:

Patterns on pages 152–53
Tracing paper
Wool: ⅝ yard dark brown,
   ⅝ yard light brown
¼ yard black felt
Dressmaker's pen
Thread to match fabrics
Polyester stuffing
Black pearl cotton
Embroidery needle
Fabric glue
2 (35-mm) wiggle eyes
1½ yards 2"-wide holiday ribbon

Note: Patterns include ¼" seam allowances.

1. Cut out patterns. Using tracing paper, transfer patterns and markings to fabrics; cut out as indicated.

2. Cut out back. To make pattern, on tracing paper draw a 14½"-diameter circle overlapped by a 12½"-

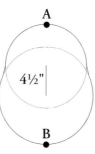

Diagram A

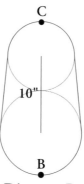

Diagram B

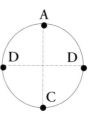

Diagram C

diameter circle, with circle centers 4½" apart (Diagram A). Connect sides with straight lines as shown. Mark center at top and bottom and label as shown. Cut out pattern along outside lines. Transfer pattern and markings to dark brown wool and cut 1; set aside.

3. Cut out front. To make pattern, on tracing paper draw an 11"-diameter circle and a 9"-diameter circle end to end, with circle centers 10" apart (Diagram B). Connect sides with straight lines as shown. Mark center at top and bottom and label as shown. Cut out pattern along outside lines. Transfer pattern and markings to light brown wool and cut 1; set aside.

4. Cut out face. To make pattern, on tracing paper draw a 12"-diameter circle. Divide it into quarters and label (Diagram C). Cut out pattern. Transfer pattern and markings to dark brown wool and cut 1; set aside.

5. Cut out legs. Draw a 4" x 17½" rectangle on tracing paper. Transfer to dark brown wool and cut out. Mark 1" from 1 short end for hoof attachment. Repeat to cut and mark 7 more leg pieces.

6. Sew legs. With right sides facing and side edges aligned, stitch 1 hoof piece to marked end of 1 leg piece. Repeat to stitch a hoof to each leg piece.

With right sides facing and raw edges aligned, sew 2 leg/hoof pieces together, leaving end opposite hoof open and a side opening for stuffing. Turn. Baste short end closed. Do not stuff leg yet. Repeat to make 3 more legs.

7. Stitch tail, antlers, ears. With right sides facing and raw edges aligned, stitch together tail pieces, leaving straight edge open. To make each ear, in same manner join 1 dark brown piece to 1 light brown piece, leaving straight edge open. For each piece, clip curves and turn. Stack antler pieces and topstitch together, leaving straight edge open and a side opening for stuffing. Set aside.

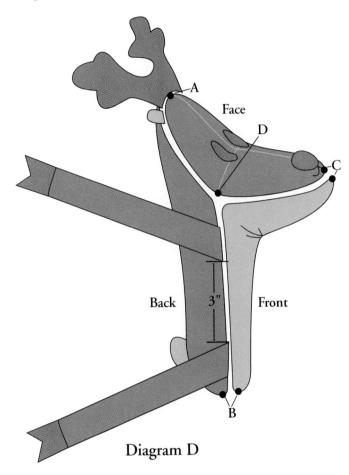

Diagram D

8. Assemble reindeer. With right sides facing and raw edges aligned, center and pin antlers to back piece at A (Diagram D); baste. In same manner, pin ears ¼" from antlers, with dark brown side down; baste.

With right sides facing and raw edges aligned, pin face to back at A and both Ds, with ears and antlers sandwiched between. Stitch pieces together, stitching from D to A to D.

With right sides facing and raw edges aligned, pin front to face at C and both Ds. Stitch pieces together, stitching from D to C to D.

With right sides facing and raw edges aligned, baste 1 leg to back just below D. Measure down 3" and baste second leg in place. Repeat on other side. Fold legs and

pin to center of back to keep them out of the way.

With right sides facing and raw edges aligned, pin front to back at Ds and Bs, with legs sandwiched between. Stitch pieces together, leaving an 8" opening at bottom for turning. Clip all seams and turn.

9. Stuff reindeer and add tail. Stuff legs, antlers, and body. Slipstitch openings closed. Slipstitch tail vertically to center bottom of back.

10. Add features. Using dressmaker's pen, transfer mouth pattern to bottom center of face. Using pearl cotton, satin-stitch mouth.

Run a gathering stitch along edge of nose piece; pull to gather slightly. Slipstitch nose to face just above mouth, stuffing just before stitching is complete.

Glue on fabric eyes. Glue wiggle eyes at bottom of each fabric piece. Tie ribbon in a bow around neck.

118

PRETTY
By Post

Turn frames, boxes, and trays into great-looking gifts. All
you need are paint, glue, and some of those stamps or postcards
you've been saving for just the right project.

Desk Accessories

Materials:
Assorted stamps
Wooden frame and papier-mâché box
Decoupage glue
Small paintbrush

1. **Decoupage stamps onto frame.** Position
stamps around frame, overlapping and wrapping
edges around sides of frame. Using paintbrush, apply
decoupage glue to backs of stamps and replace on
frame, smoothing away any excess glue. Let dry. Apply 2
or 3 coats of decoupage glue over entire surface of frame
to seal. Let dry.

2. **Decoupage stamps onto box.** Using paintbrush,
apply decoupage glue to backs of stamps and place on
box. Let dry. Apply 2 or 3 coats of decoupage glue over
entire surface of box to seal. Let dry.

Stamp Savvy *Those of the pack-rat persuasion
often can't resist collecting these miniature works of
art. But if you don't have a boxful of canceled
stamps to craft with, there are other sources.*

Hobby stores and crafts stores often sell bags
containing hundreds of foreign and
domestic stamps. Look in the section that
carries supplies for stamp collectors. On
the other hand, you can forego using
individual stamps in favor of a stamp-print
wrapping paper. To achieve a collage look with the
wrapping paper, tear the paper into small, rough-
edged pieces and decoupage the pieces to the item
you're covering. Overlap the pieces generously,
smoothing away bumps and wrinkles. For mail-
order sources for bags of stamps, decoupage glue,
and stamp-print wrapping paper, see page 156.

Tray

Materials:
Unpainted wooden tray
100-grit sandpaper
Soft cloth
Acrylic paints: cream, green
3 (2") foam brushes
Hide glue (available at hardware stores)
Assorted postcards, stamps, or other paper souvenirs
Decoupage glue
Paintbrush

1. **Prepare tray.** Lightly sand tray. Remove dust with soft cloth.

2. **Paint tray.** Using cream paint and foam brush, paint tray surface and sides. Let dry. (If wood absorbs paint, apply another coat and let dry.)

Using foam brush, apply thin coat of hide glue. Let dry.

Using green paint and foam brush, quickly paint tray surface and sides, using only 1 or 2 brushstrokes to cover. Let dry. (As paint dries, a crackle effect will appear.)

3. **Decoupage tray.** Arrange postcards and stamps on tray. Using paintbrush, apply decoupage glue to backs of all pieces and replace on tray, smoothing away any excess glue. Let dry. Apply 2 or 3 coats of decoupage glue over entire surface of tray to seal. Let dry.

READY WHEN *You Are*

These recipes serve up good taste *and* good planning.
Most of the preparation can be done the evening before.
And while the entrée bakes, you'll have time to
set the table and prepare a simple side dish.

Triple-Cheese Omelet Casserole

This savory combination of bacon, eggs, and three cheeses is reminiscent of a country omelet. Pair with piping hot biscuits for a hearty breakfast or brunch.

12 slices bacon
½ cup chopped onion
¼ cup chopped green pepper
1 (26-ounce) package frozen shredded hash browns, thawed
2 cups (8 ounces) shredded Swiss cheese
2 (3-ounce) packages cream cheese, softened
6 large eggs
½ cup milk
½ cup freshly grated Parmesan cheese
½ teaspoon salt
½ teaspoon pepper

Cook bacon in a large skillet until crisp; remove bacon, reserving 2 tablespoons drippings in skillet. Crumble bacon, and set aside.

Cook onion and green pepper in drippings over medium-high heat, stirring constantly, until tender.

Place hash browns in a greased shallow 3-quart baking dish; sprinkle evenly with Swiss cheese and half of bacon. Top evenly with vegetable mixture.

Beat cream cheese at medium speed of an electric mixer until creamy. Add eggs and milk; beat until smooth. Add Parmesan cheese, salt, and pepper; beat just until blended. Pour cream cheese mixture over vegetable mixture; sprinkle with remaining half of bacon. Cover and chill 8 to 12 hours.

Uncover and bake at 350° for 35 minutes or until set and lightly browned. Yield: 8 servings.

Sausage and Cheddar Strata

With this classic dish, you can please everyone—adults and children alike. For a complete meal, also serve broiled or fresh grapefruit halves and coffee or milk.

1½ pounds ground pork sausage
8 (1-inch-thick) slices French bread, cut into 1-inch cubes
1½ cups (6 ounces) shredded Cheddar cheese
8 large eggs, lightly beaten
2 cups milk
¾ cup half-and-half
1 teaspoon salt
⅛ teaspoon ground red pepper
⅛ teaspoon ground black pepper

Brown sausage in a large skillet, stirring until it crumbles; drain. Layer bread cubes, sausage, and cheese in a lightly greased 13- x 9- x 2-inch baking dish.

Combine eggs and remaining ingredients; pour over cheese. Cover and chill 8 to 12 hours.

Uncover and bake at 350° for 30 to 35 minutes or until set and lightly browned. Let stand 10 minutes before serving. Yield: 8 servings.

Triple-Cheese Omelet Casserole

Coconut-Pumpkin Pillow Crêpes

Try these pretty, cheese-filled crêpes for a holiday brunch or late-night Christmas supper. Enjoy them with a cup of coffee to fully savor the subtle flavors.

½ cup water
¼ cup raisins
¾ cup dried apricots
½ cup canned pumpkin
½ teaspoon grated lemon rind
2 tablespoons sugar
1 cup crumbled coconut macaroons (5 to 6 cookies)
½ cup ricotta cheese
¼ cup blanched slivered almonds, toasted and
    coarsely chopped
1 recipe Basic Crêpes
8 dried apricots
¼ cup blanched slivered almonds
2 tablespoons butter or margarine, melted
½ cup maple syrup

Combine first 3 ingredients in a 2-cup liquid measuring cup. Cover tightly with heavy-duty plastic wrap; fold back a small edge of wrap to allow steam to escape. Microwave at HIGH 3 minutes; let cool. Drain, reserving liquid in a medium saucepan. Cut apricots into thin slices. Set apricots and raisins aside.

Add pumpkin and lemon rind to liquid in saucepan; bring to a boil, stirring occasionally. Cover, reduce heat, and simmer 8 minutes, stirring occasionally. Add sliced apricots, raisins, and sugar to pumpkin mixture; bring to a boil. Reduce heat, and simmer, uncovered, 8 minutes or until thickened, stirring occasionally. Remove from heat; let cool.

Stir macaroons, ricotta, and ¼ cup toasted almonds into pumpkin mixture. Cover and chill 1 hour.

Place ¼ cup pumpkin mixture in center of each crêpe. Fold top of crêpes over filling; fold sides of crêpes over filling, and roll up crêpes. Place crêpes, seam side down, in a lightly greased 11- x 7- x 1½-inch dish. Place 1 apricot on top of each crêpe. Cover and chill 8 to 12 hours.

Cook ¼ cup almonds in melted butter in a small skillet over medium heat, stirring constantly, 2 minutes or until toasted. Stir in syrup. Transfer mixture to a glass container; cover and chill 8 to 12 hours.

Remove crêpes from refrigerator; let crêpes stand, covered, at room temperature 30 minutes. Uncover and bake at 350° for 25 minutes. Microwave syrup mixture at HIGH 2 minutes or until thoroughly heated. Serve syrup mixture with warm crêpes. Yield: 8 servings.

Basic Crêpes

½ cup all-purpose flour
⅛ teaspoon salt
½ cup plus 2 tablespoons milk
1 large egg
1 tablespoon butter or margarine, melted
Vegetable cooking spray

Combine first 3 ingredients, beating with a wire whisk until smooth. Add egg, and beat well. Whisk in butter. Cover and chill batter at least 2 hours.

Coat bottom of a 6-inch crêpe pan or heavy skillet with cooking spray; place over medium heat until hot.

Pour 2 tablespoons batter into pan; quickly tilt pan in all directions so batter covers bottom of pan. Cook 1 minute or until crêpe can be shaken loose from pan. Turn crêpe over, and cook about 30 seconds. Place crêpe on a dish towel to cool. Repeat procedure with remaining batter. Yield: 8 (6-inch) crêpes.

Chicken-Cheese Turnovers

Chicken-Cheese Turnovers *Eaten out of hand or with knife and fork, these flaky turnovers pack a flavor punch. Serve for brunch or lunch with fresh fruit or for supper with a green salad.*

½ cup minced onion

¼ cup minced celery

¼ cup minced green pepper

1 tablespoon butter or margarine, melted

2 (3-ounce) packages cream cheese, softened

½ teaspoon salt

½ teaspoon cracked black pepper

¼ teaspoon dried thyme

¼ teaspoon dried savory

3 cups chopped cooked chicken

1 (17¼-ounce) package frozen puff pastry
    sheets, thawed in refrigerator

Garnish: fresh savory sprigs

Cook first 3 ingredients in butter in a small skillet over medium-high heat, stirring constantly, until tender. Combine vegetable mixture, cream cheese, and next 4 ingredients; stir in chicken. Set aside.

Place 1 sheet of puff pastry on a lightly floured surface; roll into a 14- x 10-inch rectangle. Cut pastry into 4 (7- x 5-inch) rectangles, using a sharp knife. Spoon a heaping ⅓ cup chicken mixture onto 1 side of each rectangle; fold remaining side over mixture, and press edges with a fork to seal. Repeat procedure with remaining sheet of puff pastry and chicken mixture. Place turnovers on ungreased baking sheet. Cover and chill 8 to 12 hours.

Uncover and bake on ungreased baking sheet at 375° for 20 minutes or until puffed and lightly browned. Yield: 8 servings.

FREEZER TIP: Freeze unbaked turnovers in an airtight container up to 3 months. To bake, place frozen turnovers on an ungreased baking sheet. Bake at 375° for 30 minutes or until puffed and lightly browned.

Christmas AMONG Kindred Spirits

**For Sally Korte and Alice Strebel of Dayton, Ohio,
a design approach and the spirit of the season
go hand in hand.**

In 1988, when Sally and Alice decided to follow their friends' advice and start their own pattern company, they christened their business Kindred Spirits.

The name obviously refers to the owners—in the photograph on the facing page, Sally is on the right, Alice on the left. But, the name also suggests the lively interchange that they have fostered with customers, many of whom are now their friends.

Meaningful designs. From the beginning, Sally and Alice wanted their business to reflect their beliefs. Each of their books, pattern packets, and other products bears their motto: "May the creations of our hands be clear reflections of the Creator."

Sally and Alice have published quilts, dolls, stationery, wearables, hooked and crocheted projects, and the embroidered pieces they call "stitcheries." Though varied in medium, their works all have the primitive look for which Kindred Spirits is now widely known.

In their first book, *Gatherings,* Sally and Alice sprinkled their no-nonsense instructions with witty anecdotes, inspiring quotations, and pen-and-ink sketches.

In their second book, *Kindred Christmas,* Sally and Alice tapped even more techniques to create their designs and design variations. But they still leave the instructional material with drawings, verses, and advice.

Practice makes practical. For the crafter planning to make these designs for Christmas, Sally and Alice are quick to share their sensible take on holiday crafting.

• Don't have time to put together one of their multi-media collages? No problem. The individual design elements can be used in other ways—and in their books Sally and Alice describe dozens of them. "We encourage our readers to do what we do," they say. "Take what's given, change it, and finish it to please yourself."

• If you don't have all the materials a project calls for, try substituting something else. Not only do you save yourself a trip to the store, but you also create something uniquely yours. As Sally and Alice say, "Necessity is the mother of creative designing."

• And remember: Making things by hand is supposed to be fun. Keep experimenting with different techniques until the process is as enjoyable as the end result.

Kindred crafting. Convinced that readers of *American Country Christmas* would relish Kindred Spirits' style, we persuaded Sally and Alice to share a version of one of their appliquéd wearables. To see the Angel Vest, turn to the following pages. To find out more about Kindred Spirits and their latest offerings, see page 156.

"Appliquéing a vest is a great way to make a *holiday* garment. Since the vest is ready-made, you do the *fun* part—the embellishment."

Angel Vest *Although the vest shown has a pocket, you can also use a vest without one.*

Materials:
Patterns on page 154
Purchased denim vest
Tracing paper
Dressmaker's pen
12 (4") squares assorted gold plaid fabrics
Muslin: 1 (4 x 6") piece, 1 (4") square
4" x 6" quilt remnant or other scrap
Iron-on transfer pencil
Embroidery floss: gold, green, tan, black, red
Chenille needle
1 (2") covered button form
Trims: buttons, charms, fabric flowers (optional)
About 24 (2¼" x 12") bias strips of assorted plaid
    fabrics, joined end to end (or enough to bind all
    edges of vest)
Thread to match fabrics

Vested Interests *Sally and Alice have other ideas for perking up a purchased vest.*

   • The pieced binding alone makes a plain vest more interesting.

   • Run a garland of stars up one side, around the neck, and down the other side of a vest front.

   • In their original Angel Vest, Sally and Alice used two more appliquéd angels—one hovering above and one to the left of the stitched tree.

Note: Use 3 strands of floss for stitching muslin and gold fabric; use 6 strands for vest. For colors, refer to photo.

   1. Make appliqués. For each of 6 stars, stack 2 gold squares, wrong sides facing. Using tracing paper and dressmaker's pen, transfer star pattern to fabric. Machine-stitch along marked lines. Cut out close to stitching.

   For angel body, transfer pattern in same manner to 4" x 6" muslin. Place quilt remnant right side up with marked muslin on top; machine-stitch along marked lines. Cut out body, adding ¼" seam allowance. Cut slit in muslin, turn right side out, and press.

   For angel face, trace pattern onto tracing paper with transfer pencil. Following manufacturer's instructions, transfer pattern to center of 4" muslin square. Stitch face as indicated on pattern. (See page 141 for French knot diagram.) Cover button with design.

   2. Attach appliqués. Referring to photograph, arrange 5 stars and angel on left front of vest; pin. Attach stars with running stitches just inside edges. Slipstitch angel body in place. Sew on face. Backstitch garland (ending at shoulder seam) and wings, legs, and arms of angel.

   3. Stitch tree. Using a photocopier, enlarge tree pattern 200%. Trace pattern onto tracing paper with transfer pencil. Transfer pattern to right front of vest. Stitch tree as indicated on pattern. Attach remaining star to top of tree. If desired, attach trims to branches.

   4. Add binding. With right sides facing and edges aligned, pin binding to outside of vest. Using ½" seam allowance, stitch binding in place, overlapping ends ¾". Fold binding to wrong side of vest, turn under raw edge, and slipstitch folded edge to cover stitching line. Repeat to bind armholes.

Nested Kumquats

FRUITFUL Gifts

With fresh packaging ideas, you can put a new twist on sharing the season's abundance.

Candied Lemons Cut each of 5 small lemons into 4 wedges, cutting to, but not through, stem end. Place lemons in a quart jar so that wedges are separated. Add 4 mint sprigs, if desired; set aside. In a medium saucepan, combine 2 cups sugar and 2 cups fresh lemon juice; place over medium heat, stirring until sugar dissolves. Pour mixture over lemons in jar. Cover and refrigerate at least 1 week. Remove and discard mint; if desired, add fresh mint. To serve, flavor dessert sauces or cakes with strips of rind. Spoon the syrup over vanilla ice cream or pound cake, or stir it into hot or iced tea. Mixture will keep up to 2 months in refrigerator. Yield: 1 quart.

Wrapped Oranges Use rubber-stamped tissue paper to individually wrap juicy oranges. Present the oranges in a fruit vendor's basket or in fruit-bag netting.

Nested Kumquats An imitation bird's nest provides the perfect scale and setting for egg-shaped kumquats. To complete the picture, tuck in evergreen sprigs and wrap the whole in cellophane and ribbon.

Pear-fect Presentation Nestle several pears in a wooden crate lined with excelsior. Cassette-tape crates sold at music stores are a good size for small pears. To order pears and oranges by mail, see page 156.

Candied Lemons

Wrapped Oranges

Pear-fect Presentation

Toboggans

FOR TOTS

These colorful caps can make everybody happy. As these shining faces show,
holiday headgear is fun to wear. And since the duplicate-stitched designs work
up quickly, you'll be smiling, too.

Let It Snow

Let It Snow   *Take a tip from Mother Nature and let the snowflakes fall where they may.*

Materials:
Chart and color key on page 155
Royal blue stockinette-stitch knit cap
Straight pins
Embroidery floss (see color key)
#24 tapestry needle

Note: Finished size of each snowflake is approximately 1¾" x 1¾".

1. **Place designs.** Using pins, mark placement for 2 rows of snowflakes, centering them vertically between top of crown and top of cuff. If cap has darts, center snowflakes in top row between darts.

Hats in Hand   *Follow these tips on buying caps.*

Buy a stockinette-stitch knit cap with a gauge of 7 stitches and 9 rows to the inch. For the Santa design, you'll need a cap with a cuff at least 3" deep; for the others, a 2½"-deep cuff. For a mail-order source for the red, blue, and teal green caps, see page 156.

2. **Stitch designs.** Using 4 strands of floss, duplicate-stitch snowflakes according to chart, stitching outside layer of cap only. When finished, weave thread tail through 5 or 6 stitches on wrong side.

Father Christmas   *Keep stitches loose so that they cover but don't pucker the knit.*

Materials:
Chart and color key on page 155
White stockinette-stitch knit cap
Straight pins
Embroidery floss and metallic braid (see color key)
#24 tapestry needle

Note: Finished size of Santa is approximately 3" x 2½".

1. **Place design.** Using pins, mark placement for middle Santa, centering him vertically on cuff.
2. **Stitch design.** Using 4 strands of floss, duplicate-stitch Santa according to chart, stitching outside layer of cuff only. When finished, weave thread tail through 5 or 6 stitches on wrong side. Using 1 strand of metallic braid, stitch 1 star on each side of Santa. Repeat to stitch 1 more Santa and star on each side.

Father Christmas

O Christmas Tree

O Christmas Tree   *We used silver metallic braid for our stars, but you could substitute gold or white metallic braid or floss.*

Materials:
Chart and color key on page 155
Red stockinette-stitch knit cap
Straight pins
Embroidery floss and metallic braid (see color key)
#24 tapestry needle

Note: Finished size of tree is approximately 1½" x 1¾".

1. Place design. Using pins, mark placement for tree, centering it vertically on cuff.

2. Stitch design. Using 4 strands of floss, duplicate-stitch tree according to chart, stitching outside layer of cuff only. When finished, weave thread tail through 5 or 6 stitches on wrong side. Using 1 strand of metallic braid, stitch 1 snowflake on each side of tree according to chart. Working outward from either side, repeat to stitch more trees and snowflakes to fill cuff.

Dancing Lights   *The random placement of light bulb motifs makes it easy to work around the darts.*

Materials:
Chart and color key on page 155
Teal green stockinette-stitch knit cap
Straight pins
Embroidery floss (see color key)
#24 tapestry needle
1⅓ yards black silk cording
Black embroidery floss

Note: Finished size of each bulb is approximately 1¼" x 2".

1. Place designs. Using pins, mark placement for 2 rows of lightbulbs, centering them vertically between top of crown and top of cuff. If cap has darts, center bulbs in top row between darts about 1" below top of crown. Align bottom of bulbs in bottom row about 1" above top of cuff.

2. Stitch designs. Using 4 strands of floss, duplicate-stitch bulbs according to chart, changing floss colors as desired and stitching outside layer only. When finished, weave thread tail through 5 or 6 stitches on wrong side.

3. Attaching cording. Using 2 strands of black floss, couch silk cording to connect bottoms of bulbs.

Dancing Lights

PATTERNS

Quick Guide to Using the Patterns

Throughout this section you will find guidelines and tips for using the patterns.

Here is a list of helpful tools you may want to have on hand: tracing paper, carbon paper, dressmaker's carbon paper, a dressmaker's pen and chalk pencil, a water-soluble marker, a black felt-tipped permanent marker, a pencil, white and colored pencils, a ruler, scissors, and a craft knife.

Transferring Patterns to Fabric

The method you use for transferring the pattern will depend on the type of material to which the pattern is being transferred.

To transfer simple patterns to most any fabric, lay tracing paper on the printed pattern and trace. Cut out the traced pattern on the outline. Pin the pattern to the fabric and cut around the pattern.

For light-colored, lightweight fabric or paper, trace or photocopy the pattern. Retrace the outline with a

black marker. Tape the tracing to a window pane or light box; then tape the material over the tracing. Using a water-soluble marker, trace the pattern onto the material.

For solid or opaque materials such as dark fabric or card-stock paper, trace the pattern. Stack the material (right side up), the carbon paper (carbon side down), and the tracing of the pattern (right side up). With a dull pencil, trace over the pattern to transfer the carbon outline to the material.

Transferring Embroidery Patterns

For embroidery patterns, there are two methods: (1) Trace the design onto tracing paper. Poke holes along the outline with a pushpin. Mark over the lines with a dressmaker's chalk pencil so chalk is imprinted on the fabric. (2) Or use a hot-iron transfer pencil to trace the pattern. Following the manufacturer's instructions, transfer the pattern onto the material.

Always transfer all placement and guide markings as well as the outline to the traced pattern and material.

Flowering Fleece

Instructions are on page 20.
Patterns are full-size.

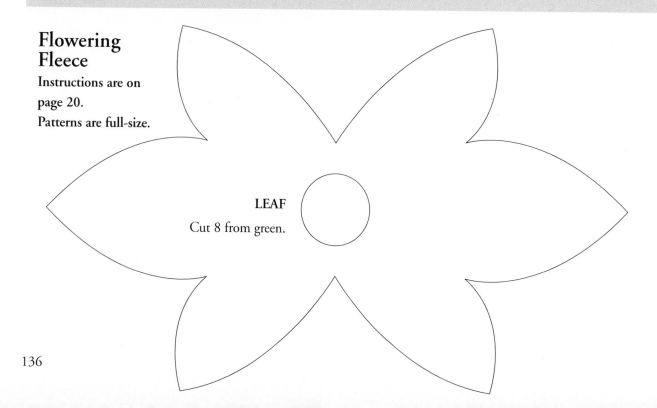

LEAF

Cut 8 from green.

FLOWER

Cut 4 from red.

Front Door Greetings

Instructions are on page 23.
Patterns are full-size.

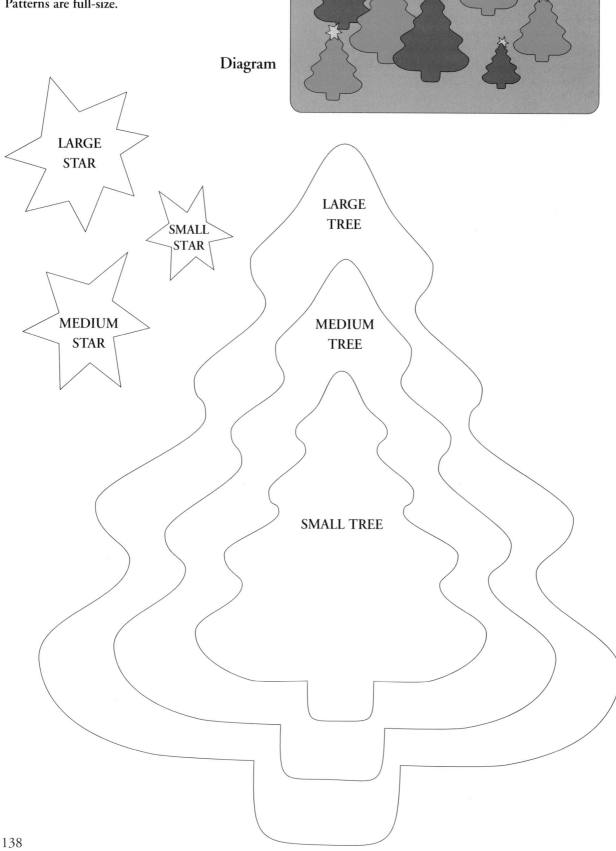

Diagram

LARGE
STAR

SMALL
STAR

MEDIUM
STAR

LARGE
TREE

MEDIUM
TREE

SMALL TREE

Stamp on the Cheer

Instructions begin on page 37.
Patterns are full-size.

JOLLY HOLLY

One Pattern, Two Looks

For a positive image, use cap of ballpoint pen to press down design areas shown in white, leaving dark areas raised. For a negative image, press down dark areas, leaving white areas raised. For a single motif, trace only 1 part of design. Cut out 1" outside design area.

SWIRLING SNOWFLAKES

DANCING TREES

HOLIDAY HOUSE

A Stitcher's Gift Instructions begin on page 43.

Getting Started
Judith Montano always begins her classes with these tips for making ribbon embroidery easier.

Threading Your Needle. To keep the ribbon from slipping, use a "needle eye lock." Referring to Diagram A, thread a 12" to 16" length of ribbon through the eye. Pierce the ribbon end and slide it down the needle to lock it in place.

Diagram A

Knotting Your Ribbon. Use a "soft knot" to knot the ribbon end. Referring to Diagram B, bring the ribbon end up to the point of the needle. Make a short running stitch in the ribbon end. Gently pull the needle and ribbon through the running stitch to form a knot.

Diagram B

Lazy Daisy Stitch

Come up at A, form a loop, and go down at B. Come up at C, bringing needle tip over ribbon. Go down at D, making a small straightstitch to anchor lazy daisy.

Decorative Lazy Daisy Stitch

First, make a lazy daisy stitch as described above. Using ribbon of a different color, come up at A and go down at C. To work a cluster of stitches, make lazy daisy stitches first; then come back and fill in with different-color straightstitches.

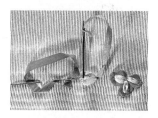
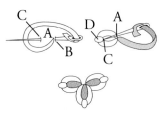

Curved Whip Stitch

Come up at A and go down at B, making straightstitch of desired length. Come up again at A. Working toward B, wrap straightstitch 2 or 3 times, pulling to curve stitch. Working back toward A, repeat wraps. To finish, pass needle to back of fabric.

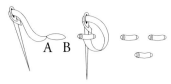

Feather Stitch

This stitch is often worked with buttonhole twist or floss. Work stitch from top to bottom. Come up at A. Go down at B and come up at C, bringing needle tip over ribbon to make a U shape. Go down at D and come up at E, making another U shape. Continue working downward. To finish, anchor with a small straightstitch.

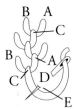

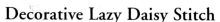

French Knot

Come up at A and wrap ribbon twice around needle. Holding ribbon taut, go down at B—as close to A as possible, but not into it. Hold knot in place until needle and ribbon completely pass through fabric.

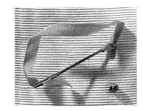

Montano Knot

This stitch is like a French knot, only bolder. Come up at A and wrap ribbon around needle 1 to 6 times, depending on desired size; keep wraps loose. Go down at B, pulling needle and ribbon though fabric without holding ribbon in place, allowing knot to be loose and flowery.

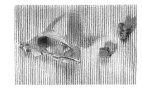

Plume Stitch

Work stitch from top to bottom. Come up at A and go down 1/8" away at B, making a loose loop. (Use a toothpick to keep ribbon flat.) Hold loop in place and come up at C, piercing loop at bottom. Continue working successive loops to finish plume.

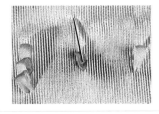

Rosette Bud

Keeping ribbon flat, come up at A and go down at B, making small straightstitch. Keeping ribbon loose, come up at C and go down at D, making padded straightstitch. Angle successive stitches to cover base of first stitch.

Japanese Ribbon Stitch

This stitch is used to make petals and leaves. Come up at A. With ribbon flat against fabric, pierce center at B. Gently pull needle through to back, keeping stitch loose. (Ribbon edges will curve at tips.) Vary stitch by adjusting length and tension of ribbon before piercing it with needle.

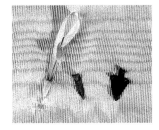

Spider Web Rose

With buttonhole twist, pearl cotton, or floss, form anchor stitch of 5 equal spokes. To form first spokes, come up at A, go down at B, and come up at C, bringing needle tip over thread; go down at D. Form 2 remaining spokes by coming up at C and going down at E, and then up at C and down at F.

To form rose, bring ribbon up at C. Working counterclockwise, weave ribbon under and over spokes. Keeping ribbon loose and allowing it to twist and curve, continue weaving until spokes are completely covered.

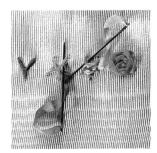 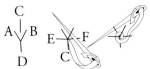

A Stitcher's Gift

Instructions begin on page 43.
Patterns are full-size.
* Note: All patterns are reversed for use
with iron-on transfer pencil.

Stitch Key

⬮	Japanese Ribbon Stitch
∘	French Knot
↷	Curved Whip Stitch
⊕	Spider Web Rose
⬖	Rosette Bud
ⵋ	Feather Stitch–floss
⬙	Lazy Daisy Stitch
⬙	Decorative Lazy Daisy Stitch
⬭	Montano Knot
⬳	Plume Stitch

Top

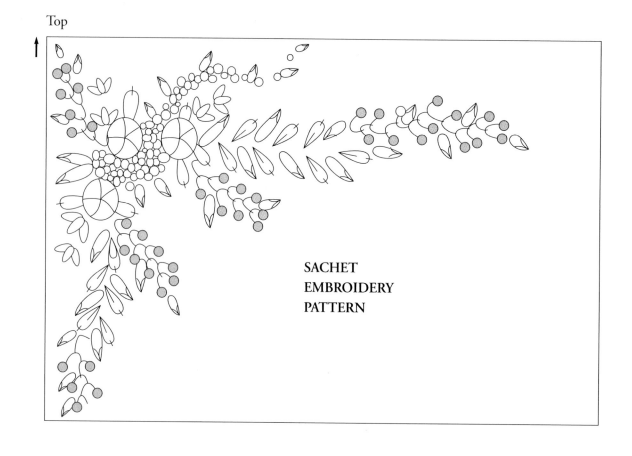

SACHET
EMBROIDERY
PATTERN

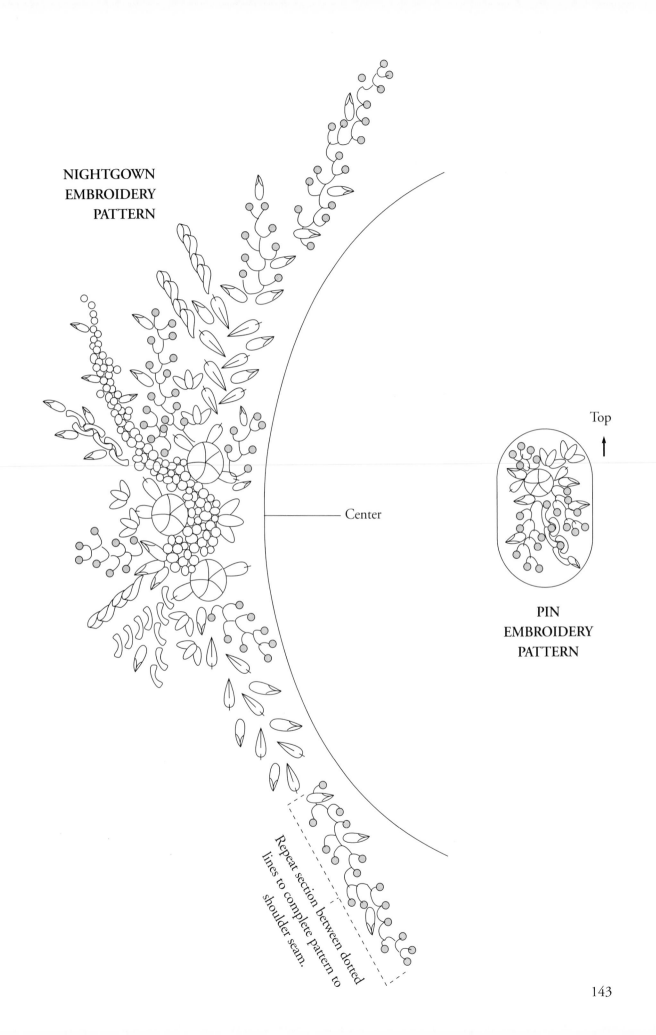

**NIGHTGOWN
EMBROIDERY
PATTERN**

Top

Center

**PIN
EMBROIDERY
PATTERN**

Repeat section between dotted lines to complete pattern to shoulder seam.

143

Stylish Slippers

Instructions begin on page 48.
Patterns are full-size and
include ⅝" seam allowance.

Instructions begin on page 48.

Toe-ing the Line

• **Watch your step.** For slip-proof slippers, add a few zigzags of dimensional fabric paint to the slipper bottoms.

• **Sizing it up.** For perfect sizing, you may want to create your own slipper pattern. Simply trace the foot and use our patterns as a guide for slipper curves, adding ⅝" for seam allowance. For an even easier method, reduce or enlarge our printed pattern on a copy machine.

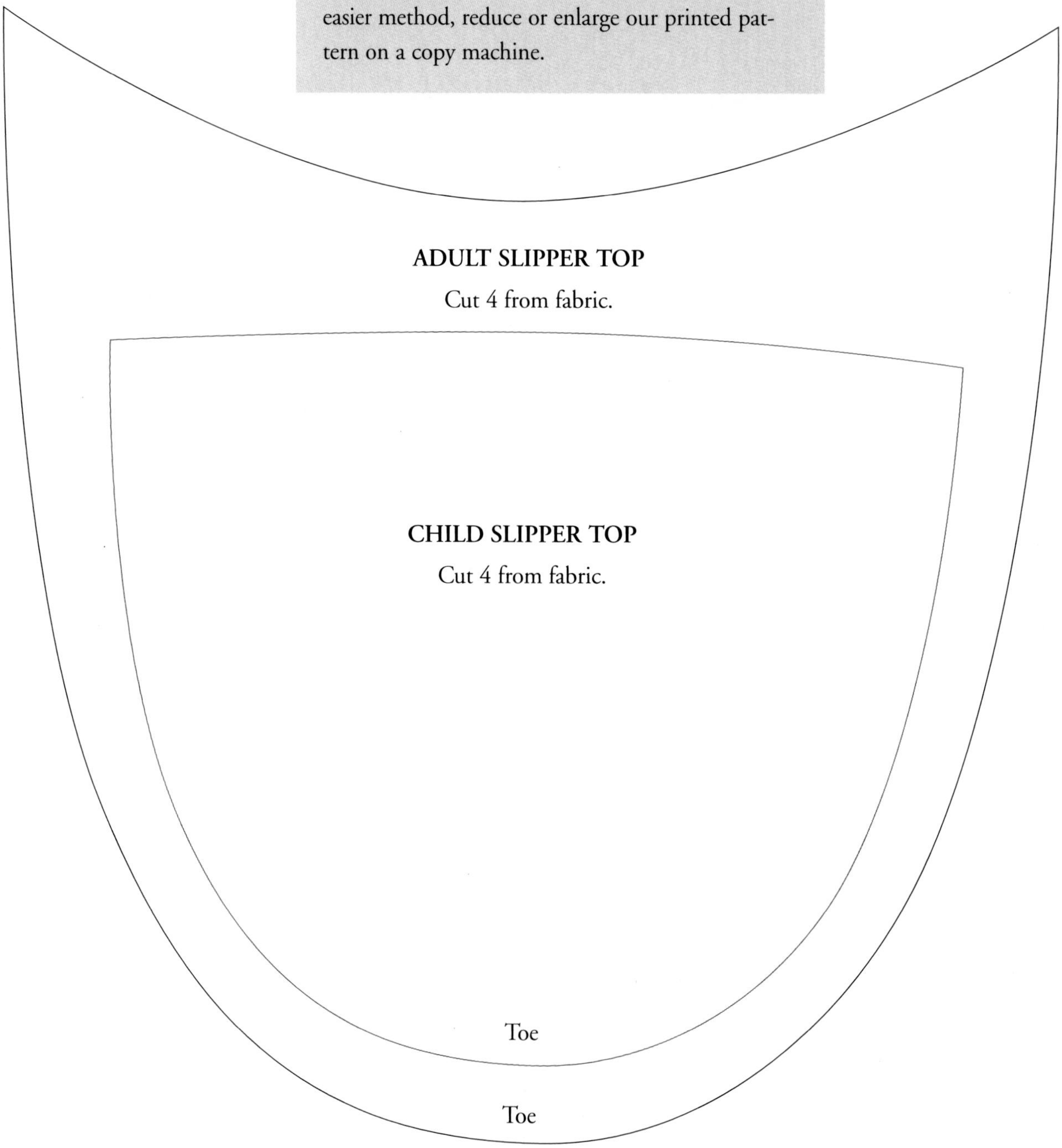

ADULT SLIPPER TOP

Cut 4 from fabric.

CHILD SLIPPER TOP

Cut 4 from fabric.

Toe

Toe

Toe

CHILD SLIPPER
BOTTOM

Cut 4 from fabric.

Cut 2 from foam.

Match dots for
complete pattern
for adult slipper
bottom.

Toe

ADULT SLIPPER
BOTTOM

Cut 4 from fabric.

Cut 2 from foam.

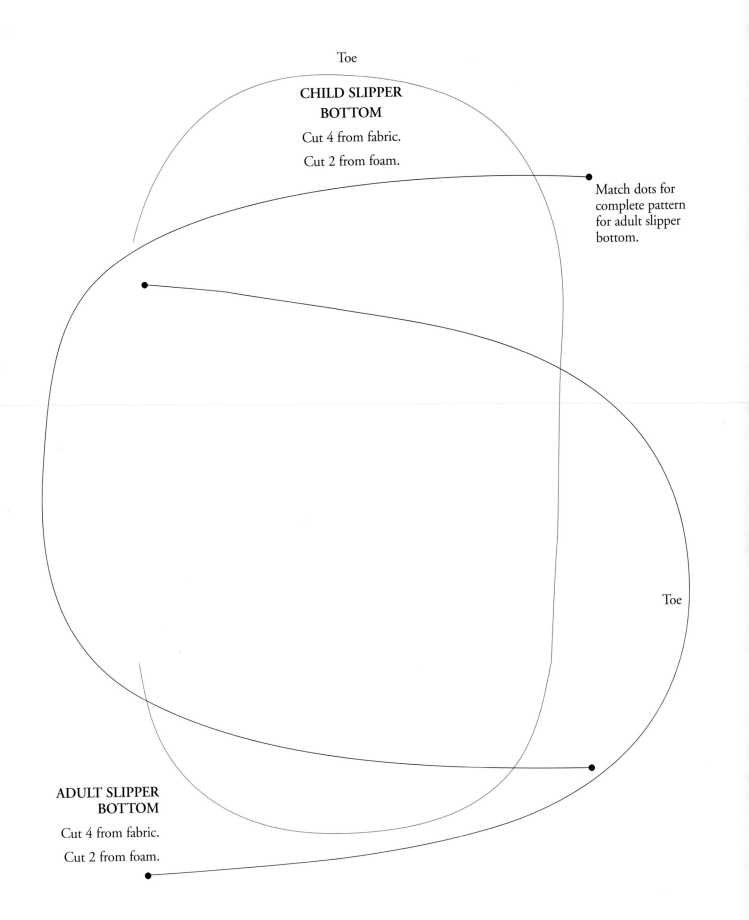

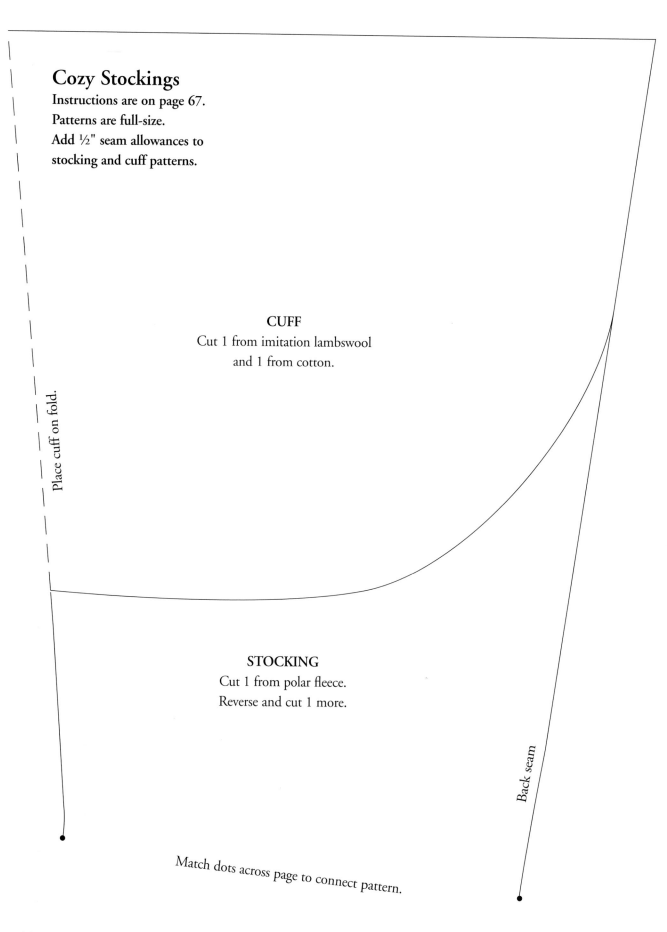

Cozy Stockings

Instructions are on page 67.
Patterns are full-size.
Add ½" seam allowances to
stocking and cuff patterns.

Place cuff on fold.

CUFF
Cut 1 from imitation lambswool
and 1 from cotton.

STOCKING
Cut 1 from polar fleece.
Reverse and cut 1 more.

Back seam

Match dots across page to connect pattern.

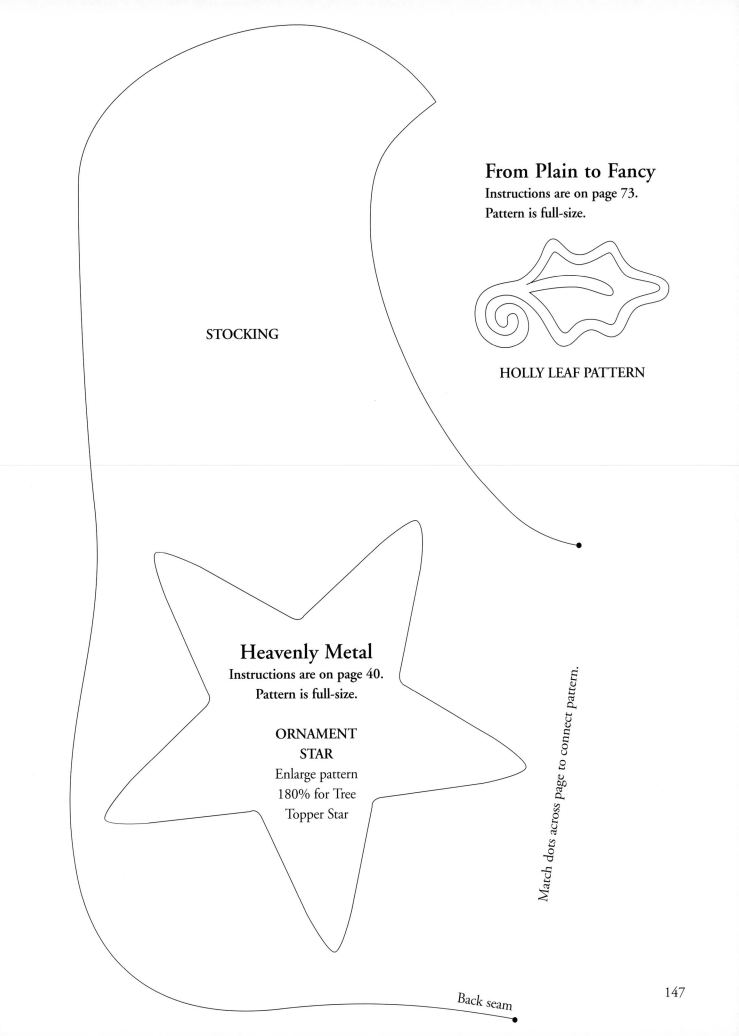

STOCKING

From Plain to Fancy
Instructions are on page 73.
Pattern is full-size.

HOLLY LEAF PATTERN

Heavenly Metal
Instructions are on page 40.
Pattern is full-size.

ORNAMENT
STAR
Enlarge pattern
180% for Tree
Topper Star

Match dots across page to connect pattern.

Back seam

Santa at Your Service

Instructions are on page 80.

* Note: Images are reversed.

A Glass Act
Instructions are on page 92.
Pattern is full-size.

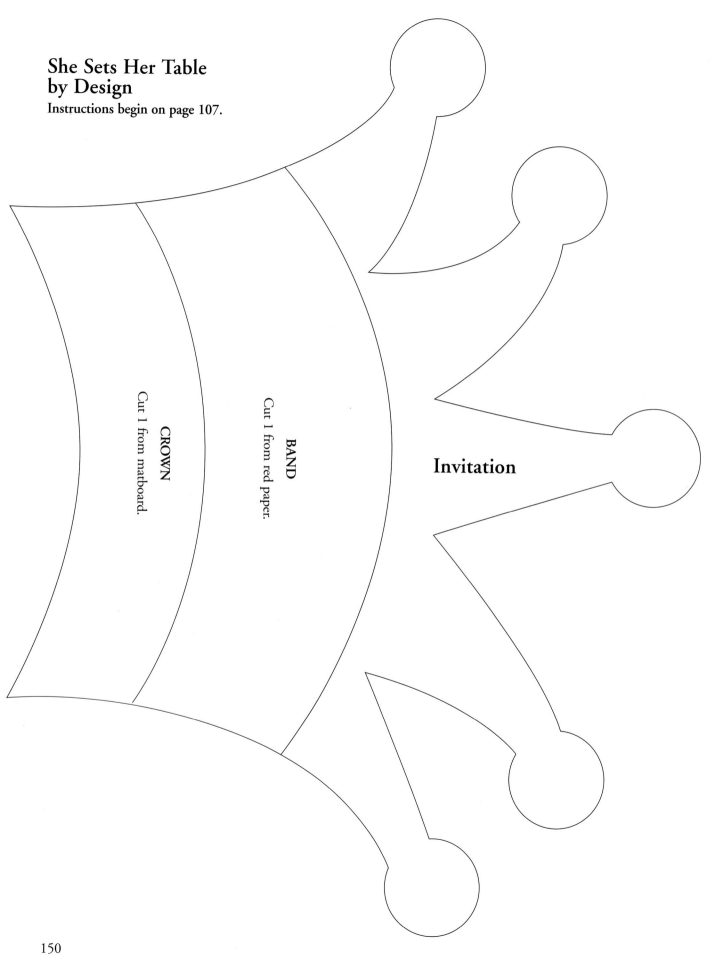

She Sets Her Table
by Design
Instructions begin on page 107.

CROWN
Cut 1 from matboard.

BAND
Cut 1 from red paper.

Invitation

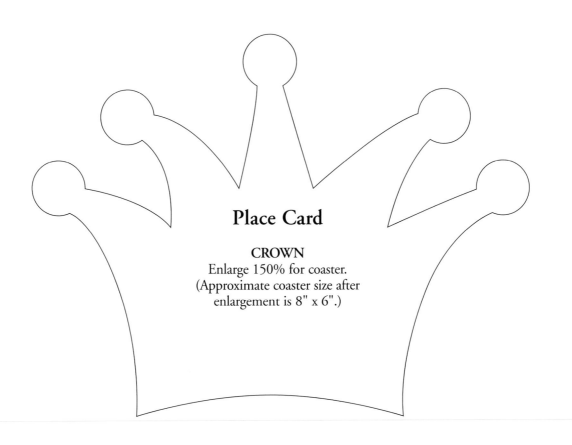

Place Card

CROWN
Enlarge 150% for coaster.
(Approximate coaster size after
enlargement is 8" x 6".)

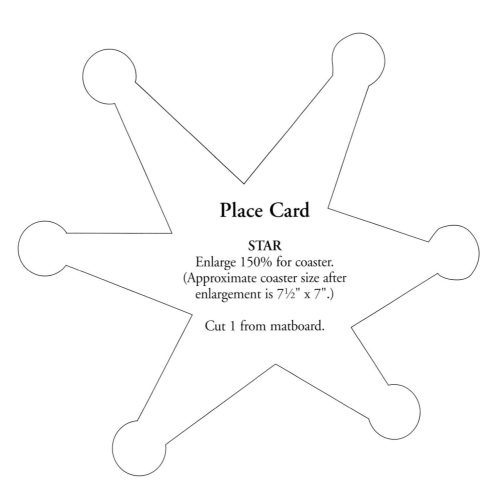

Place Card

STAR
Enlarge 150% for coaster.
(Approximate coaster size after
enlargement is 7½" x 7".)

Cut 1 from matboard.

Reindeer Pal

Instructions begin on page 116.
Patterns are full-size and include
¼" seam allowances.

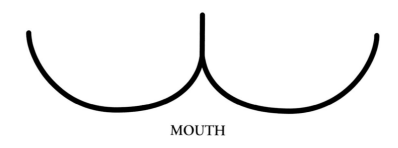

MOUTH

EYE
Cut 2 from black felt.

Stitch this edge to bottom of leg.

HOOF
Cut 8 from black felt.

Stitching line

NOSE
Cut 1 from black felt.

Gathering line

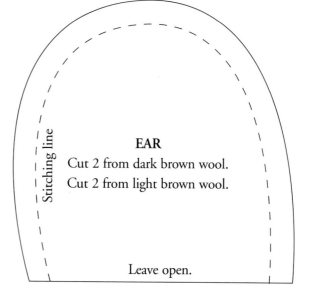

Stitching line

EAR
Cut 2 from dark brown wool.
Cut 2 from light brown wool.

Leave open.

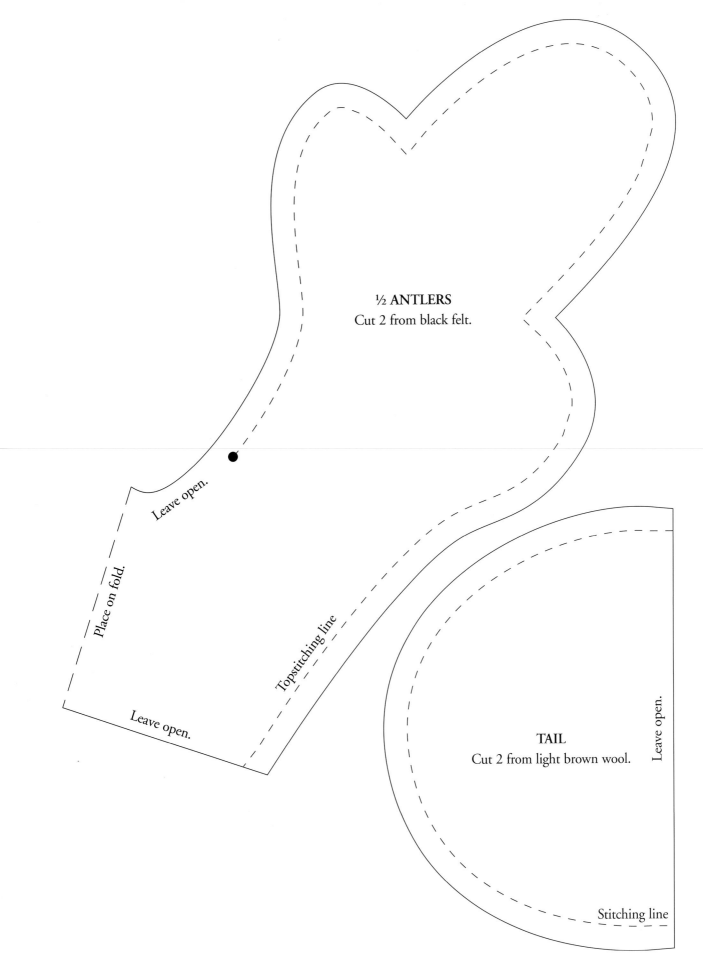

½ **ANTLERS**
Cut 2 from black felt.

Leave open.

Place on fold.

Leave open.

Topstitching line

TAIL
Cut 2 from light brown wool.

Leave open.

Stitching line

Christmas Among Kindred Spirits

Instructions begin on page 128.

Patterns are full-size.

TREE

Enlarge pattern 200%.

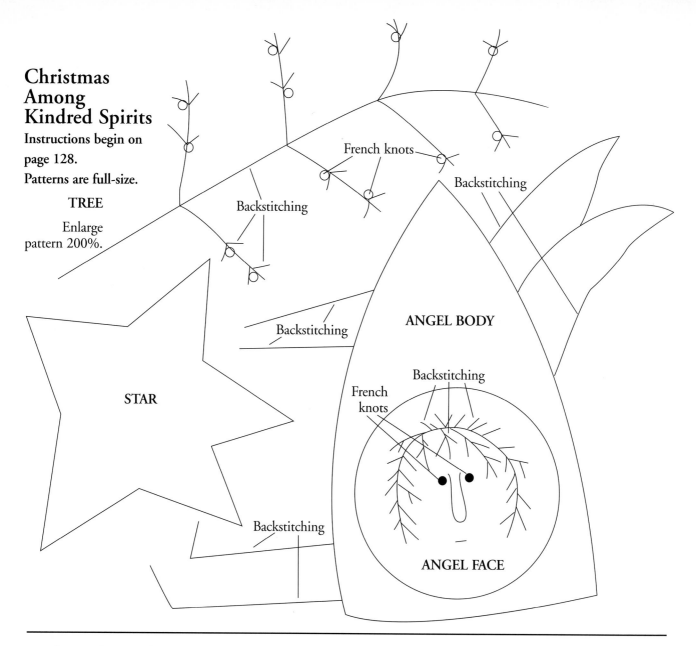

French knots

Backstitching

Backstitching

STAR

ANGEL BODY

Backstitching

Backstitching

French knots

ANGEL FACE

Backstitching

Backstitching

Celestial Candles to Light Up the Season

Instructions are on page 57. Patterns are full-size.

STENCILED CANDLES

Cut out.

Cut out.

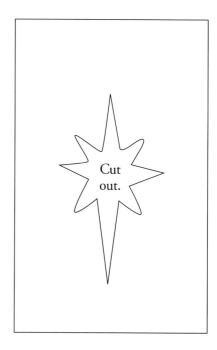

Cut out.

Toboggans for Tots

Instructions begin on page 134.

How to Duplicate-Stitch

Each square on graph represents 1 duplicate stitch. Thread tapestry needle with floss and bring up through fabric from back to front at A.

Insert needle at B and pull floss through. Bring needle back through A to wrong side.

Complete Row, working from right to left. If vertical row of stitches is required, stitch from top to bottom.

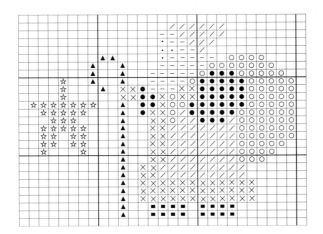

Diagram A   **Diagram B**   **Diagram C**

Note: Unless otherwise noted, numbers in color keys are for DMC floss. For numbers of strands to use, see color keys.

Father Christmas

Step 1: Duplicate stitch

- ■ 310 Black (4 strands)
- − 318 Steel gray lt. (4 strands)
- ● 498 Christmas red very dark (4 strands)
- / 666 Christmas red bright (4 strands)
- ○ 783 Topaz (4 strands)

- ▲ 801 Coffee brown dark (4 strands)
- · 951 Cream (4 strands)
- ✕ 3818 Emerald green ultra very dark (4 strands)
- ☆ 002HL Gold Kreinik #8 fine braid (1 strand)

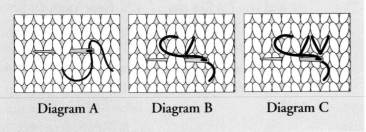

Dancing Lights

Step 1: Duplicate stitch

- ■ 782 Topaz med. (4 strands)
- ♡ Alternating, as desired: 208 Lavender medium, 444 Canary deep, 666 Christmas red bright, 907 Parrot green light (4 strands)

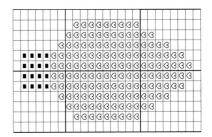

O Christmas Tree

Step 1: Duplicate stitch

- ● 701 Kelly green (4 strands)
- ✕ 001 Silver Kreinik #8 fine braid (1 strand)

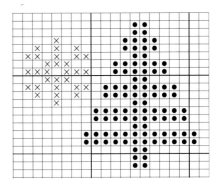

Let It Snow

Step 1: Duplicate stitch

- ✕ White 1 (4 strands)

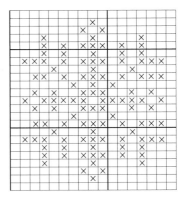

SOURCES

Stamp projects, page 119

• Page 8—eyelash fringe: M's Fabric Gallery, 200 S. 21st Street, Birmingham, AL 35233; or call (205) 323-7755 or (800) 467-3065.

• Page 11—star-figured net: For free catalog, contact Calico Corners, 3663 Lorna Road, Birmingham, AL 35216; or call (205) 988-5533.

star-figured laces: Prelude Lace and Twinkle Lace in Waverly's Lace Coordinates Collection; call (800) 423-5881 for the Waverly source nearest you.

• Page 12—wreaths: Laurel Springs Christmas Tree Farm, P.O. Box 85, Laurel Springs, NC 28644; or call (800) 851-2345.

naturals: For free catalog, contact Tom Thumb Workshops, P.O. Box 357, Mappsville, VA 23407; or call (804) 824-3507.

• Page 18—boxwood by the pound: Laurel Springs Christmas Tree Farm, P.O. Box 85, Laurel Springs, NC 28644; or call (800) 851-2345.

crinkle wire and trims: For catalog, send $3 to D. Blümchen & Company, P.O. Box 1210-ACC, Ridgewood, NJ 07451-1210; or call (201) 652-5595.

charms: Creative Beginnings, P.O. Box 1330, Morro Bay, CA 93443; or call (800) 367-1739.

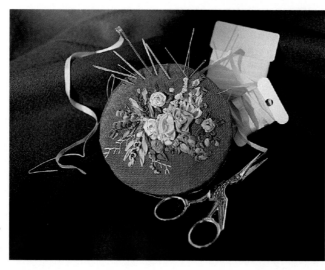

Silk ribbon embroidery, page 43

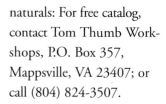

• Page 27—essential oils: For catalog, send $2 to Sunfeather Herbal Soap Company, 1551 State Hwy. 72, Potsdam, NY 13676; or call (315) 265-3648.

essential oils: Caswell-Massey Co., Ltd., 121 Fieldcrest Ave., Edison, NJ 08837; or call (800) 326-0500.

essential oils: For free catalog, contact The Essential Oil Company, P.O. Box 206, Lake Oswego, OR 97034; or call (800) 729-5912.

spices, both whole and ground, for cooking and crafting: For free catalog, contact Spices, Etc., P.O. Box 5266, Charlottesville, VA 22905; or call (800) 827-6373.

naturals: For free catalog, contact Tom Thumb Workshops, P.O. Box 357, Mappsville, VA 23407; or call (804) 824-3507.

• Page 34—puzzles: Bits & Pieces, 1 Puzzle Place-B8016, Stevens Pt., WI 54481; or call (800) JIGSAWS.

• Page 40—wire: The Beadery Craft Products, P.O. Box 178, Hope Valley, RI 02832; or call (401) 539-2432.

• Page 42—To order books and videotapes by Judith Baker Montano, contact C & T Publishing, P.O. Box 1456, Lafayette, CA 94549; or call (800) 284-1114.

• Page 43—silk ribbon and embroidery supplies: Nancy's Notions, P.O. Box 683, Beaver Dam, WI 53916-0683; or call (800) 833-0690.

silk ribbon and embroidery supplies: Cotton Patch, 1025 Brown Ave., Lafayette, CA 94549; or call (510) 284-1177.

• Page 57—candle-making supplies: Pourette Manufacturing Co., P.O. Box 17056, Seattle, WA 98107; or call (206) 789-3188, or fax (206) 789-3640.

Stenciled candles, page 57

candle-making supplies: For catalog, send $2 to The Barker Company, 15106 10th Ave. SW, Seattle, WA 98166; or call (800) 543-0601.

• Page 60—Papier-mâché boxes with frame lids: Kel-Toy, Inc., 255 Barneveld Ave., San Francisco, CA 94125; or call (415) 641-4885.

• Page 63—Ribbon: Smith Variety, 2715 Culver Road, Birmingham, AL 35223; or call (205) 871-0841.

ribbon: Midori, Inc., 3524 West Government Way, Seattle, WA 98199; or call (206) 282-3595.

• Page 67—polar fleece: For catalog, send $5 to Thorburn's, 123 Nashua Road, Suite 128 AC, Londonderry, NH 03053; or call (603) 437-4924.

imitation lambswool: For samples, send $5 to Monterey, Inc., 1725 E. Delavan Dr., Janesville, WI 53545; or call (800) 432-9959.

• Page 72—glass ornaments: Smith & Hawken, 2 Arbor Lane, Box 6900, Florence, KY 41022; or call (800) 776-3336.

• Page 76—reproduction vintage ornaments: Vinny's Showplace, 1076 South Colony Rd., Wallingford, CT 06492; or call (800) 98VINNY.

reproduction vintage ornaments: For catalog, send $15 to Margo's Gift Shop, 2058 Yorktown Alley, Tulsa, OK 74114; or call (800) 886-2746.

Greenery swag, page 76

reproduction vintage ornaments: Christmas at the Zoo, 118 N.W. 23rd Ave., Portland, OR 97210; or call (800) 223-5886. Catalogs available.

Fruit gift ideas, page 130

• Page 95—velvet: Waverly Town & Country velvet in hunter, cherry, and nugget; call (800) 423-5881 for the Waverly source nearest you.

• Pages 106–8—acrylic gems, hand-printed velvets, and coasters: Angèle Parlange Design, 5419 Magazine St., New Orleans, LA 70115; or call (504) 897-6511.

• Page 108—candles: Susan Schadt Designs, 2120 Jimmy Durante Boulevard, Suite 108, Del Mar, CA 92104; or call (800) 459-4595.

• Page 112—satin ribbon and photo albums: Smith Variety, 2715 Culver Road, Birmingham, AL 35223; or call (205) 871-0841.

• Page 119—canceled stamps: Lenox Stamp and Coin, 3393 Peachtree Road N.E., Atlanta, GA 30326; or call (404) 266-3166.

decoupage glue: For a catalog, send $3 to Schrock's International, 110 Water St., Bolivar, OH 44612; or call (330) 874-3700.

stamp-print wrapping paper: For free catalog, contact City Paper Co., P.O. Box 1968, Birmingham, AL 35201; or call (205) 328-2626 or (800) 621-9989.

• Page 126—For complete catalog on Kindred Spirits' books, pattern kits, and stationery, send $3 to Kindred Spirits, 115 Colonial Lane, Dayton, OH 45429; or call (513) 435-7758.

• Page 130—fresh fruit by mail: For free catalog, contact Harry and David, P.O. Box 712, Medford, OR 97501; or call (800) 547-3033.

• Page 134—knit caps: For free catalog, contact Lands' End, 10 Lands' End Lane, Dodgeville, WI 53595; or call (800) 356-4444.

INDEX

GENERAL

RECIPES

CONTRIBUTORS

CRAFT DESIGNERS

Alice L. Cox,
slippers, 48–49
Janice Cox,
potpourri recipes and
packaging, 26–29
Charlotte I. Hagood,
Christmas cardigans,
50–53
Margot Hotchkiss,
candles, 56–57; woven
ribbon photo albums,
112–13
**Kindred Spirits (Sally Korte
and Alice Strebel),**
folk art designs, 111,
126–29
Heidi T. King,
wire stars, 30, 40–41;
cocktail napkins, 79,
80–81
Judith Baker Montano,
silk ribbon embroidery,
42–47
Barbara McNorton Neel,
puzzle mat, 34–35
Dondra Green Parham,
bead garlands, 31–33;
foam stamps, 36–39
Angèle Parlange,
invitations, place cards,
napkin wraps, party
favors, 104–9
Carol S. Richard,
boxwood topiaries, 4–5,
18–19; wreaths, 12–15
Betsy Cooper Scott,
doormat, 22–23; burlap
plant wrappers, 24–25;

bows, 62–65; painted
glassware, 92–93;
reindeer, 114–17
Carole Sullivan,
greenery swag, 74–77
Cynthia M. Wheeler,
mantel swag, 10–11;
wool throws, 16–17;
fleece table linens, 20–21
Peggy Ann Williams,
polar fleece stockings, 54,
66–67; Christmas card
projects, 58–61; wine
bags, 94–95
Lois Winston,
duplicate-stitched caps,
110, 132–35

RECIPE DEVELOPERS

Debbie Maugans,
coffee recipes, 78, 102–3;
dinner menu recipes,
84–91
Angie Sinclair,
sauce recipes, 79, 82–83;
cookie recipes, 96–101
Elizabeth Taliaferro,
make-ahead meal recipes,
122–25

PHOTOGRAPHERS

All photographs were taken
by **John O'Hagan** except
the following:

Ralph Anderson,
68, 71, 78, bottom 79,
82–83, 84–90, 97–101,
102–3, 123, 125
Gary Clark,
74–77
Chris Little,
inset 42, inset 45, inset
46
Peter Woloszynski,
104–9

PHOTO STYLISTS

All photographs were styled
by **Katie Stoddard** except
the following:

Margo Bouanchaud,
104–9
Virginia Cravens,
68, 71, 78, bottom 79,
82–83, 84–90, 97–101,
102–3, 123, 125

SPECIAL THANKS

• Thanks to the following
talented people:

Barbara Ball
Johnny Cain
Jazmyn Denson
Kent Essinger
Grace Ann Hollis
Nick and Hope Howard
Neely Jones
Joey Long
Jennifer Mathews
Kathy Mathews
Susan Ray
Ernest Sheely
Lauren Wright

• Thanks to the following
homeowners:

John and Jane George,
Blount Springs, AL
Linda and Kneeland Wright,
Birmingham, AL

• Thanks to the following
businesses:

Dollywood,
Pigeon Forge, TN
Interiors Market,
Birmingham, AL
Laurel Springs Christmas
Tree Farm, Laurel
Springs, NC